The Art
of
Painting
on
Silk

Volume 3
Fashions

The Art
of
Painting
on
Silk

Volume 3
Fashions

Edited by Pam Dawson
Translated by Kate Horgan

Search Press

First published in Great Britain 1989
Search Press Ltd
Wellwood, North Farm Road,
Tunbridge Wells, Kent TN2 3DR

This book has been rewritten and rearranged from original
French editions of *Peinture sur Soie* © Les Éditions de Saxe –
Peinture sur Soie 1985, 1986, 1987

English version *The Art of Painting on Silk Volume 3 – Fashions*
copyright © Search Press Limited 1989

The designs shown in this book are created by the
following artists: pages 7, 87 Gervaise; 9, 11, 15, 16, 17, 21,
25, 27, 31, 35, 37, 39, 43, 49, 51, 53, 55, 58, 59, 61, 63, 65, 67,
70, 74, 75, 76, 77, 81, 83, 85, 91, 93, 94, 103, 105 Joelle
Dreville; page 12 Catherine d'Angeli; pages 19, 28, 33, 57,
71, 97, 99, 109, 111 Akane Kinu.

Translated by Kate Horgan

ISBN 0 85532 628 X

Converting centimetres to inches

centimetres	inches
1.25	½
2	¾
2.5	1
3	1¼
3.5	1⅜
4	1½
4.5	1¾
5	2
5.5	2⅛
6	2¼
6.5	2½
7	2¾
7.5	3
8	3¼
8.5	3⅜
9	3½
10	4
20	7¾
30	11¾
40	15¾
50	19¾
60	23½
70	27½
80	31½
90	35½
100	39½

Typeset by Scribe Design, 123 Watling Street, Gillingham,
Kent.
Made and printed in Spain by Salingraf S.A.L. Bilbao

CONTENTS

Introduction

The third volume of this highly successful series 'The Art of Painting on Silk' combines the luxury of pure silk with original hand painted designs and French fashion flair. No other material produces such beautiful effects when combined with modern silk paints. Even the amateur can achieve excellent results. It has always been regarded as one of the most luxurious of fabrics and when complemented with an original hand-painted design it has a sheen and glow quite unlike anything which is machine manufactured.

This book will inspire the experienced artist to explore a new medium and enable the complete beginner to tackle an exciting craft. The techniques are really very simple. It is not necessary to possess drawing skill and colour sense as might be expected, so much as patience and diligence. With these two qualities the basic skills of painting on silk can easily be mastered.

Here there are many colourful examples of beautiful and elegant garments, both for adults and children. There is a wide selection of fashion designs, from scarves and lingerie to blouses and jackets. Each design is shown in full colour, together with details of the materials required, examples of the methods used and a simple-to-follow chart of the painted motif.

Silk is produced by the silkworm. A cultivated silkworm feeds only on mulberry leaves and at one stage of its evolution it spins a cocoon of very fine, elastic thread which can be as much as 3,000 metres, or nearly 10,000 feet in length. This thread is very strong and although it is woven into fabrics which may appear delicate, they will stand up very well to normal wear and tear, although not to excessively rough handling. When choosing a fashion garment, therefore, the designs should emphasize the softness of silk with flowing lines.

Silk was produced in Italy in the twelfth century and in France the first silk was woven in the sixteenth century. Painting on silk, which was by then highly developed in the Far East, was taken up in France and French techniques and style came to influence the rest of the Western world. Sadly the art declined in popularity and was forgotten until early in the present century, when it was rediscovered in southern France and Brittany.

Although silk painting is not an exorbitantly expensive hobby it is certainly not cheap for, of course, silk is a precious material. Nor can it be guaranteed that your first attempt will be a masterpiece. If you are a complete beginner it is best to start with a small design on a remnant of silk, which can be used as a decorative handkerchief. Once you begin to experiment, however, you will soon discover what a wealth of possibilities the craft has to offer. The garments featured in this book will offer something suitable for all skills and will inspire you to create your own uniquely original designs.

Opposite: Gossamer silk and delicate painting make this the dress for the wedding of your dreams. See pages 88 and 89 for instructions.

Silk scarves

If you are reluctant to test your skill at painting complex designs, or undertaking more intricate dressmaking projects, then the ideal way to begin painting on silk is by making one of the delicate scarves featured in this section.

A silk scarf complemented with an original design painted in luminous colours deserves to be finished in the best possible way. Some of the garments shown in this book automatically have their edges concealed by various seaming methods, but this is not possible when completing a scarf, as the edges remain visible.

Straight, machine hemming can be used; it is quick and easy but not really worthy of a luxury item. A rolled hem gives the neatest finish and can be worked in one of two ways; either by machine and hand, or entirely by machine using a narrow foot hemmer.

Hand-rolled hem: make sure all the edges of the silk are perfectly straight. Allow a total of 1cm/½in on all edges for the finished rolled hem. Work a staystitch by hand, or with small machine stitches, 3mm/⅛in from the raw edges, all round the scarf. Trim the fabric away to within a few threads of the staystitch, (see Fig a).

Turn the full hem allowance to the wrong side and roll the raw edge under so that the line of staystitching just shows. Thread a fine sewing needle with thread of the same colour as the silk and work from right to left along the hem.

Sew along the hem with small, loose blind stitches - these are similar to slip stitches - working through the staystitching and the edge of the scarf. Make several stitches and then gently pull up the slack in the thread, causing the edge to roll under, (see Fig b). Do not press the rolled edges, which should be left softly rounded. This is what gives a hand-rolled hem its characteristic appearance.

Machine-rolled hem: trim the edges to allow 1cm/½in hem, making sure they are perfectly straight. To hold the hem in place, turn under 6mm/¼in and gently press along the foldline with your fingers. Turn under the remaining hem allowance to form a double hem and press with your fingers in the same way, lightly tacking the hem in place as you go.

To complete the hem, slip it into place under the hemmer foot of the machine and stitch in place, (see Fig c). Remove the tacking and press very lightly.

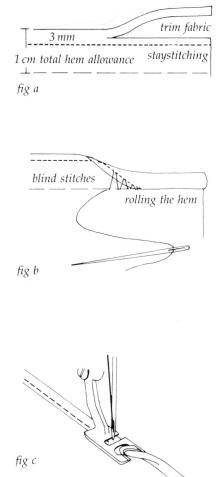

3 mm

trim fabric

1 cm total hem allowance   staystitching

fig a

blind stitches

rolling the hem

fig b

fig c

machine stitching with a hemmer foot

Opposite: Long, elegant chiffon scarves are ideal accessories. See overleaf for instructions.

Long chiffon scarves

These scarves measure 135cm/54in long by 46cm/18in wide when finished, see page 9 for illustration.

Materials

Fabric: lame chiffon 140cm/55in long by 48cm/19in wide.

Paints: amethyst, navy blue, ruby, wine red, bright pink for pink scarf.

Rosewood, dark brown, chrome yellow, gold yellow, vermillion, jade, leaf green for yellow scarf.

Dark brown, leaf green, old gold, duck egg blue for turquoise scarf.

Combinations of these colours as well as diluted versions.

Gutta: gold.

Method examples

Prepare the pots with different colours for use. To paint the background, use a thick, soft brush or large piece of cotton wool.

Pink and turquoise scarves: paint the background, and leave to dry. Draw the motif with gold gutta, then apply the paints to the centre of each circle.

Yellow scarf: Draw the motif with gold gutta and paint the centre of each circle, then cover the outlines with paraffin wax. Paint the background, then carefully wipe off the tiny drops of colour formed on the paraffin wax and iron under a piece of white absorbent paper, such as blotting paper, until the silk becomes soft again.

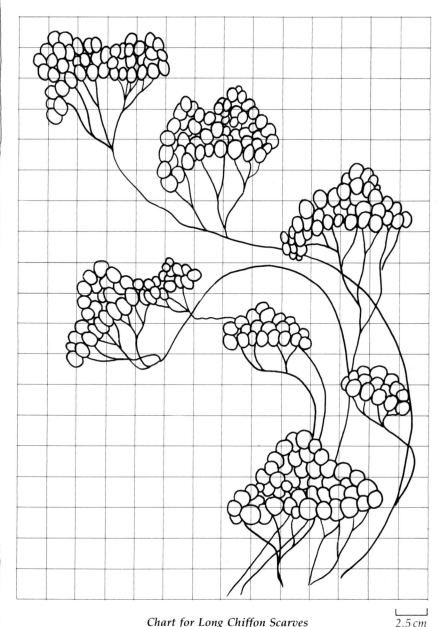

Chart for Long Chiffon Scarves

2.5 cm

Orchid scarf

This scarf measures 91cm/36in square when finished.

Materials

Fabric: silk twill 94cm/37in square.

Paints: pink, chrome yellow, yellow-gold, old gold, tangerine, cobalt blue, jade, rosewood and combinations of these colours as well as diluted versions.

Gutta: colourless.

Method examples

The flowers remain very pale. Dampen them with a mixture of

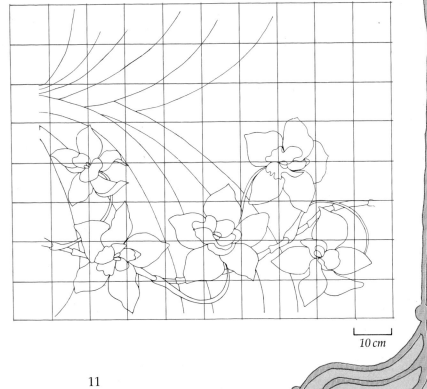

Above: Rich jade green and cobalt blue form the ideal background for these delicate orchids.

water and alcohol, slightly dilute the pink, then apply in thin brush-strokes to leave trails. Add shading with very diluted rosewood. Paint the flower centres in yellow tones, blending well with the shadows. Use tangerine for the centre pistils.

Dry well and cover the surface of the flowers with fixative. Leave to dry. Paint in pink and rosewood spots on the petals and smaller rosewood spots on the centres.

Barely shade the stalks with a little very diluted jade and rosewood.

Paint the background in alternate bands of jade and cobalt blue.

10 cm

11

Flowers of the field scarf

This scarf measures 88cm/35in square when finished.

Materials

Fabric: crepe de chine 91cm/36in square.

Paints: scarlet, wine red, yellow-gold, tangerine, cobalt blue, azure blue, rosewood, leaf green, jade, black and combinations of these colours as well as diluted versions.

Gutta: colourless, add black for the poppy and daisy stamens, dark brown for the corn ears, green for the foliage.

Method examples

Draw the motif with gutta and when completely dry, paint in the background with a small sponge and a mixture of water, alcohol and a few drops of rosewood to obtain a cream background. Leave the daisies white. When the background is dry, paint in the flowers.

Poppies: for the petals, use unmixed, diluted scarlet and wine red; shade well and brighten up with a few touches of yellow-gold and tangerine.

Daisies: shade the petals lightly with grey; use very diluted tangerine and rosewood for the centres.

Cornflowers: paint the majority in cobalt blue, lightened here and there with water and alcohol; use azure blue for the remainder to add contrast. Paint some of the centres in tangerine and the others in yellow-gold.

Corn ears: use tones of rosewood and yellow-gold, slightly diluted and mixed to give each grain a different colour.

Foliage: paint in a range of greens obtained from leaf green, jade and black. Darken some leaves with a mixture of jade and black; lighten others with leaf green and diluted jade.

Ribbon and bows: paint in pure cobalt blue.

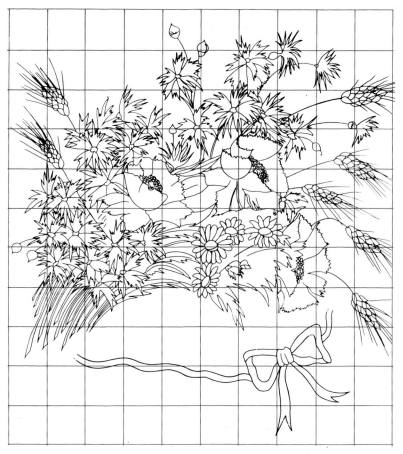

5.5 cm

12

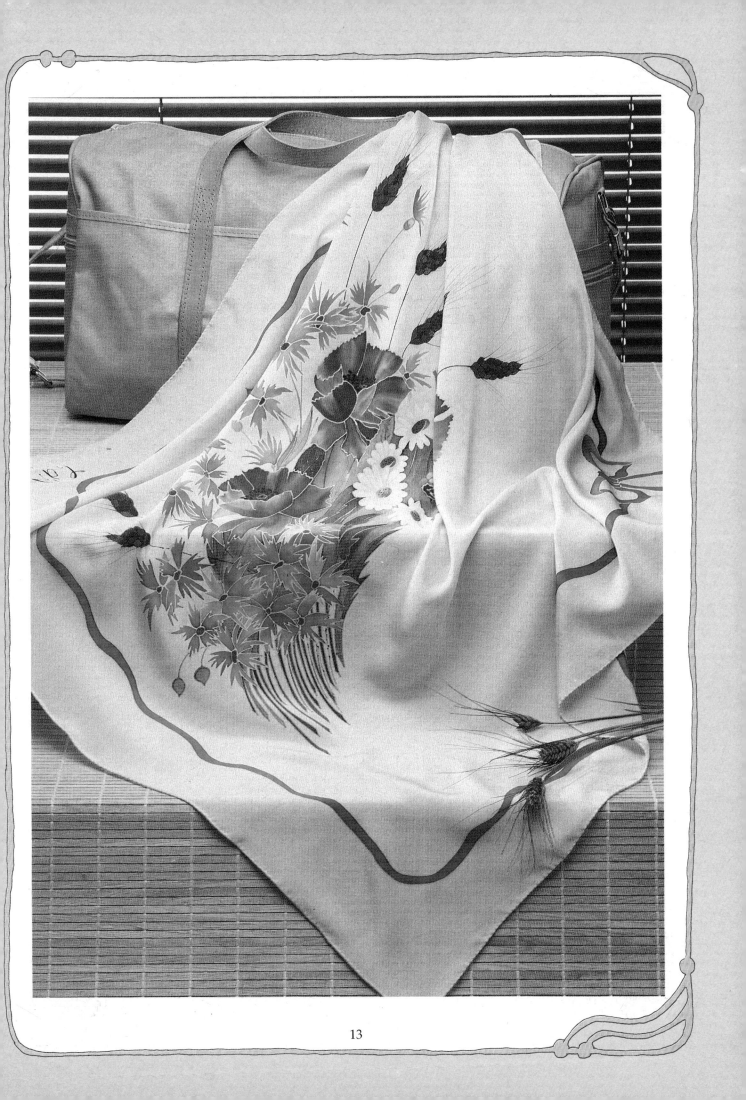

Butterfly scarf

This scarf measures 91cm/36in square when finished.

Materials

Fabric: silk twill 94cm/37in square.

Paints: pink, fuchsia, chrome yellow, tangerine, azure blue, cobalt blue, black, amethyst, duck egg blue, jade, leaf green and combinations of these colours as well as diluted versions.

Gutta: black and green; use black for the butterflies and green for the foliage and borders.

Method examples

The foliage is painted in a mixture of leaf green and jade, sometimes lightened with yellow, or darkened with a little black or blue, used pure or diluted.

The wings of the butterflies are shaded by placing small strokes of colour side by side and then, when this is almost dry, touching up with a little alcohol to give a scale-like appearance.

The background is pure cobalt blue. When completely dry add large, irregular touches of water.

The inner border is very diluted chrome yellow; the outer border is slightly diluted pink.

Opposite: Deep, dramatic colours are used to paint a riot of butterflies on this scarf. The background is mottled with spots of alcohol.

5 cm

Long random patterned scarf

This scarf measures 140cm/55in long by 40cm/16in wide when finished.

Materials

Fabric: silk twill 142cm/56in long by 43cm/17in wide.

Paints: pink, fuchsia, amethyst, azure blue, cobalt blue, jade, duck egg blue, chrome yellow, black and combinations of these colours as well as diluted versions.

Gutta: pink.

Method examples

Draw the pattern twice along the length of the scarf. Paint in the areas of colour as shown, used either pure or mixed and diluted to various strengths. Only the yellow is not applied pure but should be mixed with diluted duck egg blue to give a pale, green-yellow.

Shade the inside of some of the circles; for example, pink with amethyst shading. Use water or alcohol, or a contrasting colour to shade inside other outlines, while the surface is still a little damp.

The background is grey-blue. Apply touches of pink, blue and pale green-yellow while the surface is still damp.

Left: Water or alcohol have been used to achieve the mottled background on this delicate scarf.

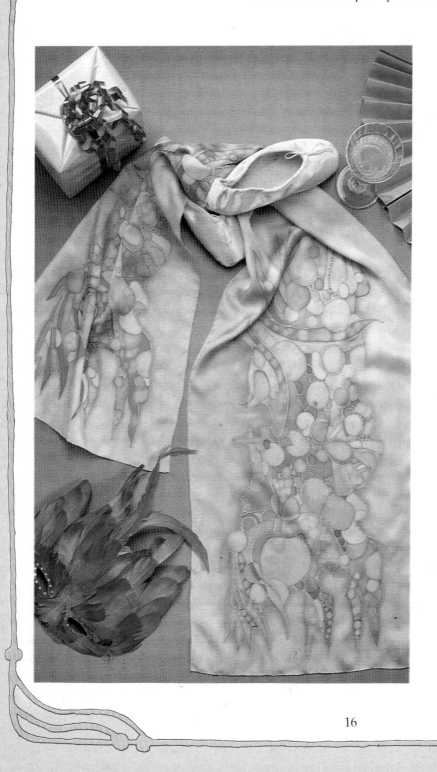

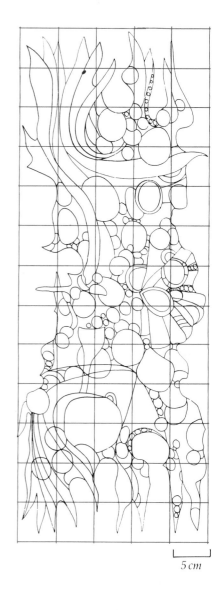

5 cm

Random patterned scarves

These scarves measure 76cm/30in long by 23cm/9in wide when finished.

Materials

Fabric: white silk 79cm/31in long, by 26cm/10¼in wide.

Paints: your own choice.

Method examples

These examples do not have any gutta lines and the paints are allowed to flow into each other.

Apply the colours in whatever manner pleases you. From time to time, place some water/alcohol solution directly on to the silk. Blend by rubbing so that the shades mix. Apply salt as you go along.

When everything has dried, brush off the salt. Make a few spots with alcohol if you wish.

Right: These long scarves show how paints can flow into each other. The unusual mottled effects are achieved by applying salt or water and alcohol.

Roses scarf

This scarf measures 88cm/35in square when finished.

Materials
Fabric: crepe de chine 91cm/36in square.

Paints: ruby red, olive green, leaf green, wine red, rosewood, black and combinations of these colours as well as diluted versions.

Gutta: colourless.

Method examples
Use mixtures of both greens to colour the leaves. Shade the flowers in mixtures of ruby red and darken them with rosewood or pale grey.

Paint the background in grey.

For the inner border use diluted ruby red; for the outer, wine red mixed with black. Allow to dry and then paint on a second coat.

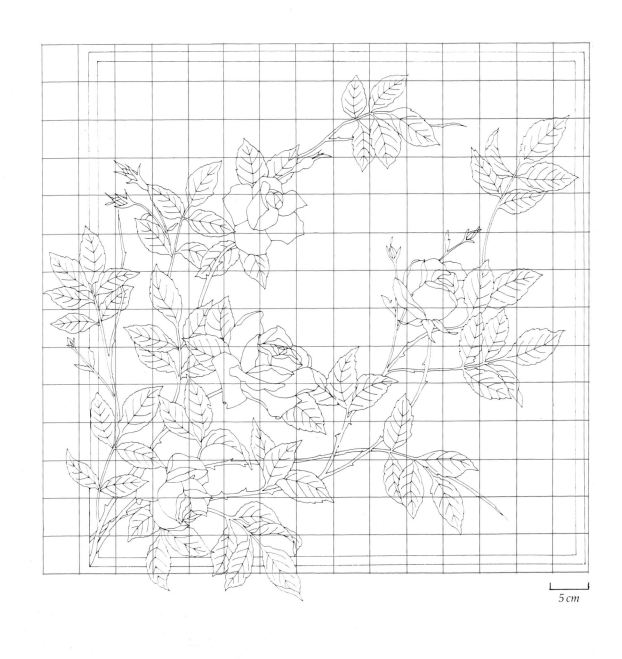

5 cm

Opposite: Full-blown roses decorate this square scarf, which is edged with a wide border of wine red.

Silk lingerie

The most sensuous of all uses for pure silk is as hand-made lingerie. Add to this an original hand-painted design and you have garments of unsurpassed luxury. Having perfected your skill at painting on silk, however, you must also have some basic knowledge of dressmaking techniques before attempting any of the designs featured in this section. The following hints will be useful in producing perfect results.

Delicate fabrics need careful handling, both at the making up stage and in their after-care. To launder, handwash all garments and gently roll in a colour-fast towel, smoothing out the creases and allow to partly dry. Iron at the recommended setting while the fabric is still damp.

The seams and hems on lingerie must not be too bulky and the machine stitches should be kept as small as possible to avoid the risk of puckering the fabric. Where necessary, fine dressmaking pins should be used as these will not mark the fabric. Use the special threads which are available for working on silk materials.

Bias bound edges

The simplest way of neatening the armholes and neckline on a night-dress or camisole is with bias binding, cut from the same fabric. To cut fabric for binding, the bias edge needs to be at an angle of 45 degrees from the selvedge. To obtain this, place the piece of fabric so that one cut straight edge is level with the selvedge and pin them together. The fold of the fabric now indicates the true bias, (see Fig a).

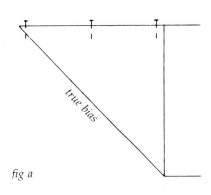

fig a

Cut the required number of bias strips needed to bind the edges, approximately 2.5cm/1in wide. Mark out each extra strip from the fold line, (see Fig b).

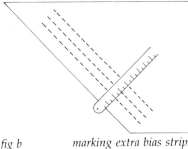

fig b   marking extra bias strips

Where two strips need to be joined to complete the binding of an opening, pull a thread at the joining end of both strips and cut across the straight grain of the fabric. With the right sides facing, place one strip on top of the other so that the bias edges cross each other about 6mm/¼in from the pointed ends. Stitch the ends together 6mm/¼in in from the edges, (see Fig c).

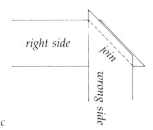

right side   *join*   *wrong side*

fig c

To bind raw edges: have the right side of the bias strip and the edge of the garment facing each other. Machine the edges together 6mm/¼in in from the edge, (see Fig d).

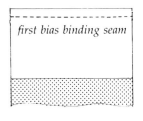

first bias binding seam

fig d

Turn to the wrong side, fold under 6mm/¼in hem and hem-stitch by hand along the first line of machine stitching, (see Fig e).

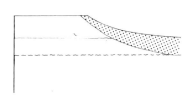

fig e   completing bias binding edge

Rouleau tubes

This method can also be used to neaten an opening, sewing the rouleau in place along the edge after the raw edges have been secured with a line of machine zig-zag stitches. The best use for rouleau, however, is as dainty shoe-string shoulder straps cut from the same fabric.

To make a rouleau tube, cut a strip 2.5-3cm/1-1¼in wide from the true bias of the material as explained above. With the right sides facing each other, fold the

Opposite: *Luxurious silk pyjamas are teamed with a matching dressing gown. See overleaf for instructions.*

strip in half lengthwise and machine the edges 6-8mm/¼-⅝in in from the edge, (see Fig f).

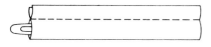

fig f   seaming a rouleau tube

Make sure that the turnings are the same width as the tube as they make the filling for the rouleau. Lightly stitch the end of the tube to the eye of a blunt-ended sewing needle, (see Fig g).

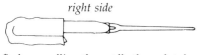

fig g   stitching a needle eye in place

Pull the needle through the tube until it comes out at the other end, (see Fig h). Remove the needle from the tube and neaten the two short ends.

right side

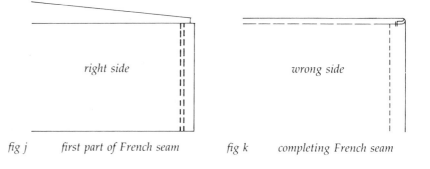

fig h   pulling the needle through tube

French seams

This method should be used on sheer fabrics, where the raw edges cannot be oversewn, either by hand or with machine zig-zag stitches, to prevent them fraying.

With the wrong sides of the two pieces of fabric to be joined facing each other, tack along the edge 1.5cm/⅝in in from the edge.

right side

fig j   first part of French seam

Machine stitch just outside the tacking line, (see Fig j). Remove the tacking and trim the fabric to just under 6mm/¼in.

Turn, so that the right sides of the fabric are facing each other and tack and machine the seam so that the raw edges are enclosed, (see Fig k).

wrong side

fig k   completing French seam

Dressing gown and pyjamas

To fit an 86-91cm/34-36in bust and 91-97cm/36-38in hips. See page 21 for illustrations.

Materials

Fabric: from self-striped silk/satin cut the following pieces:-

Dressing gown: from 71cm/28in wide fabric cut 2 lengths of 120cm/48in; cut one in half for fronts and shape front V-neck and keep other piece for back, allowing an extra 4cm/1½in for hems and extra for seams, (or required length).

From 50cm/20in wide fabric cut 2 lengths of 43cm/17in for sleeves, allowing an extra 15cm/6in for turned-back cuffs and extra for seams, (or required length).

From 10cm/4in wide fabric cut 2 lengths for front bands, to fit up front edges and meet at centre back neck, allowing extra for seams.

From 10cm/4in wide fabric cut 178cm/70in for belt, allowing extra for seams, (or required length).

Cut 2 pockets approximately 20cm/8in square, allowing extra for seams.

Pyjama tunic: from 66cm/26in wide fabric cut 2 lengths of 58cm/23in for body, as pattern below, allowing an extra 4cm/1½in for hem and extra for seams, (or required length).

From 50cm/20in wide fabric cut 2 lengths of 30cm/12in for sleeves, allowing 4cm/1½in for hems and extra for seams, (or required length).

Bias binding strip for neckband.

Pyjama trousers: from double thickness of fabric cut 2 front and 2 back pieces, as shown in pattern. Cut facings.

Paints: pink, ruby red, fuchsia, cobalt blue, azure blue, duck egg blue, black, yellow-gold, old gold, rosewood and combinations of these colours as well as diluted versions.

Gutta: pink.

Method examples.

Reproduce the entire pattern on the back of the dressing gown and on the front of the pyjama tunic.

Draw the lamp on the right-hand dressing gown pocket and let the smoke drift up on the right front of the dressing gown. Draw the flowers only on the left front of the gown.

Use all the colours very well diluted, except the black for the

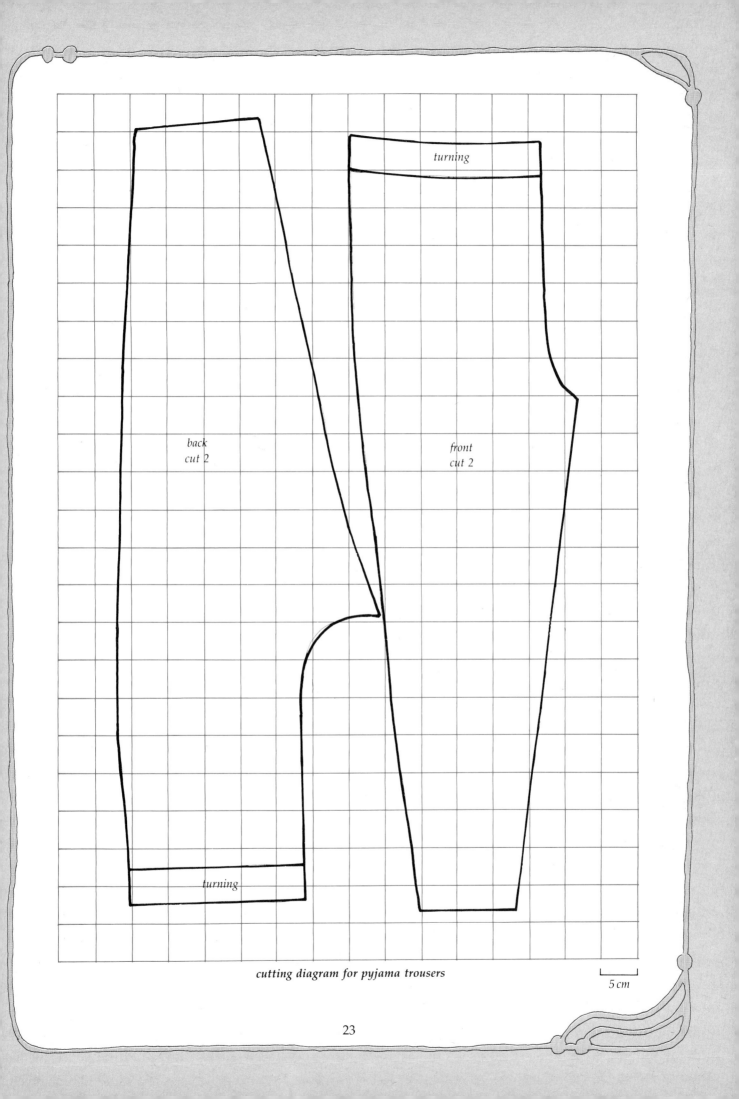

back
cut 2

front
cut 2

turning

turning

cutting diagram for pyjama trousers

5 cm

hair - this is lightened with a few touches of duck egg blue.

Shade and blend the flower colours. Paint the veil in rosewood and very diluted yellow, keeping it slightly lighter at the edges so that it appears transparent.

To make up the dressing gown

Join shoulder and side seams. Join sleeve seams, reversing lower edge for turned-back cuff. Sew in sleeves.

Join short edges of front bands so that seam forms centre back neck. With right sides facing each other, sew front band in place, fold in half to wrong side and stitch in place. Turn up hem at lower edge.

Sew on pockets, making sure that the lamp is aligned with the first trails of smoke on front. Make tie belt.

To make up pyjamas

Join shoulder and side seams of tunic, then join sleeve seams and set in sleeves. Turn hems to wrong side and stitch in place. Sew bias binding border round V-neck edge.

Place the trouser fronts on top of the backs, with right sides facing each other. Tack, then join side seams.

Fold trouser legs lengthwise, with right sides facing each other. Tack and then sew inside leg seams as far as crutch.

Place the trouser legs together, with right sides facing each other and one leg inside the other. Begin at top of back and tack down back, round crutch and up front, then sew seam.

Tack, then sew the facing to the top of the waistband. Stitch a small length of elastic, about 15cm/6in or as required, across both side seams. Fold facing down and stitch in place.

Turn trouser leg hems to wrong side and stitch in place.

chart for pyjamas and robe

6 cm

Nightdress with arabesque motif

Make this nightdress to suit your own measurements and to your own pattern.

Materials

Fabric: satin.

Paints: pink, scarlet, black and combinations of these colours as well as diluted versions.

Gutta: black, colourless.

Method examples

Draw the design on the front of the nightdress at the top of the neck and along the front edge of the side slit.

Use black gutta for all the outlines and colourless gutta for the background design indicated by faint black lines on the chart.

Paint the patterns in black and grey, leaving white spaces.

The background should be very pale. Use a mixture of water and alcohol mixed with a few drops of scarlet and pink.

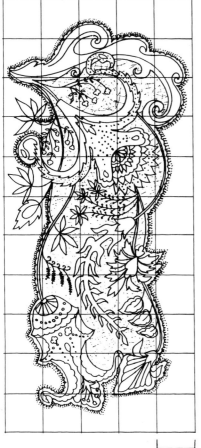

3.5 cm

Above: The rich sheen of satin makes an ideal background for this interesting motif.

Flowered nightdress

This nightdress fits an 86-91cm/34-36in bust.

Materials

Fabric: silk crepe 91cm/36in wide, 2 pieces cut to the required length as the pattern below and allowing extra for hem. Satin bias for border on V-neckline, armholes and shoulder straps.

Paints: ruby red, yellow-gold, jade, duck egg blue, tangerine and combinations of these colours as well as diluted versions.

Gutta: pink for the flowers and pale green for the stems and leaves.

Method examples

Draw the pattern in bands across the width of the fabric, once in one direction, then in the other, turning the traced design round for each band. Copying the whole design on to tracing paper the same size as the fabric will help you be more accurate with the placing of the motifs.

Use a range of diluted greens to paint the leaves. The flowers are painted with diluted ruby red, with a touch of diluted tangerine in the centres.

To make up

Join the side seams. Sew the satin bias border to the V-neckline at back and front.

Sew a satin bias border around each armhole, beginning beneath the arm and folding the border over on itself for 25cm/10in, or length required, to form shoulder straps.

Hem the lower edge.

Opposite: A demure nightdress with satin bindings is liberally patterned with dainty posies.

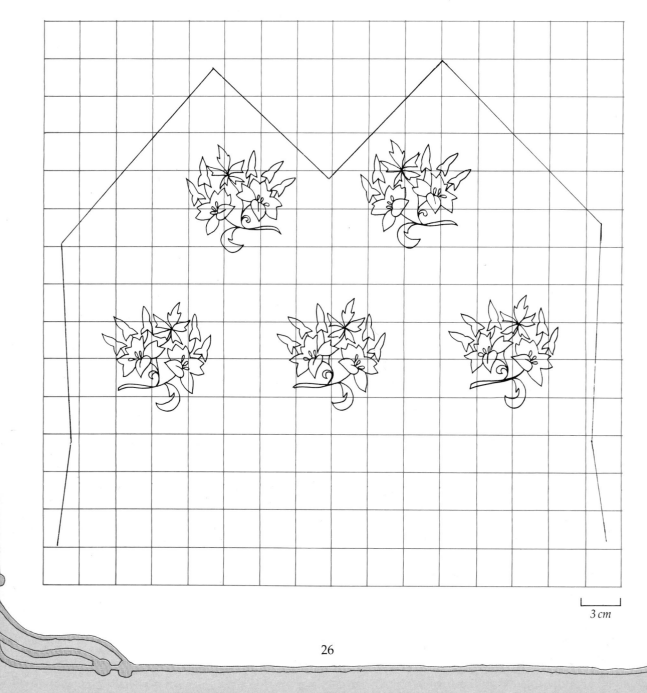

3 cm

House robe with peacock motif

This design is illustrated as an at-home robe but it is pretty enough for evening wear. It is for the experienced needlewoman and the instructions do not include details for assembling the pieces. This model fits an 86cm/34in bust.

Materials

Fabric: approximately 360cm/142in length of 91cm/36in wide silk crepe de chine for robe; approximately 300cm/118in length of 91cm/36in wide Habotai lining; approximately 140cm/55in length of 30cm/12in silk chiffon for sleeves.

Paints: duck egg blue, turquoise, leaf green, Venetian red, Indian brown, ruby red, scarlet and combinations of these colours as well as diluted versions.

Gutta: colourless.

Method examples

Draw the motif on the lower edge of the front skirt. Leave the background white

Flowers: dilute and mix some scarlet and ruby red. Blend and shade the colours when applying.

Peacock: the body and tail are painted in duck egg blue, turquoise, Venetian red and Indian brown, used practically pure for the head and wings and diluted for the tail fan. When the surface is almost dry, paint the feathers. Use pure colours and apply with a fine brush.

Peahen: paint the body in Venetian red and the tail in Indian brown and scarlet, using the colours pure.

Foliage: use a mixture of duck egg blue, turquoise and leaf green for the leaves, shading well.

28

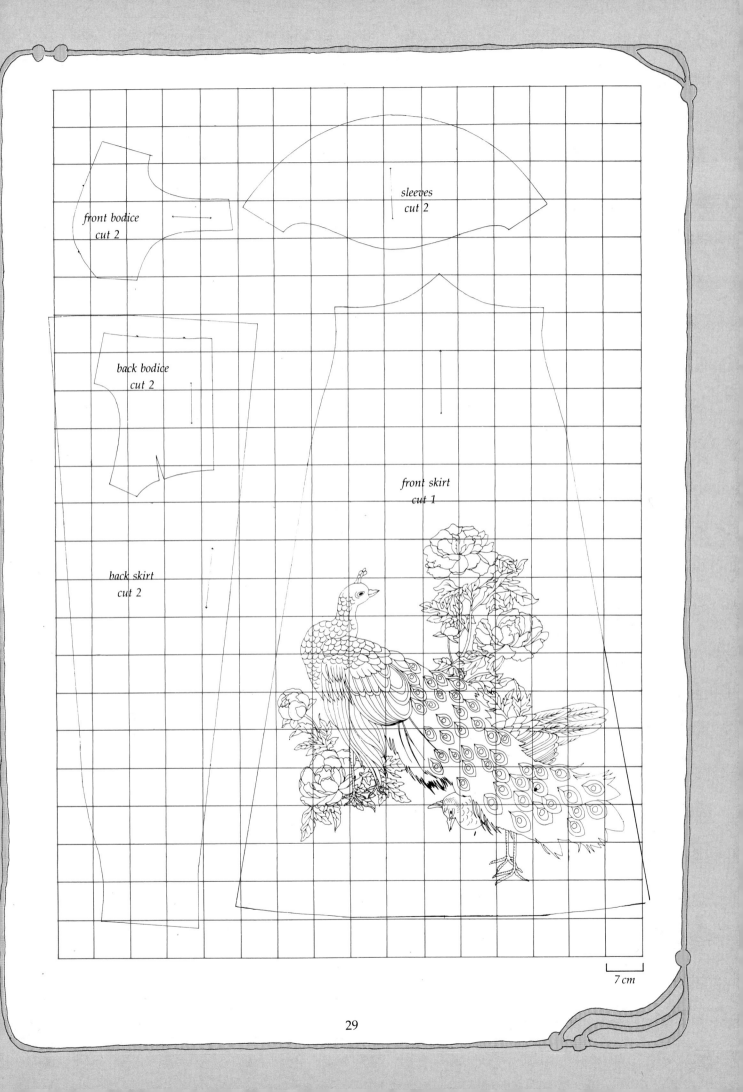

front bodice
cut 2

sleeves
cut 2

back bodice
cut 2

front skirt
cut 1

back skirt
cut 2

7 cm

Short nightdress

This nightdress fits an 91cm/36in bust.

Materials

Fabric: silk satin 60cm/23in wide, 2 pieces 91cm/36in long, or required length, allowing extra for hem.

Paints: wine red, yellow-gold, azure blue, duck egg blue and combinations of these colours as well as diluted versions.

Gutta: pale yellow and pale blue.

Method examples

The pattern is identical for the back and front. Trace the design on the front, with the smaller flower at the top. Apply the gutta, alternating the blue and yellow. Leave the background white.

Paint the design, using all the colours very diluted. The large blue petals are worked in azure blue and duck egg blue. Make them a little darker at the base and tinged with a few strokes of pink.

The pink petals are worked in diluted wine red and should also be darker at the base. Shade with a little pale blue, occasionally adding a touch of pale yellow.

For the leaves and stems use azure blue and a touch of very pale yellow.

To make up

Cut a strip of bias from the satin and tack along the front and back neckline. Sew in place, fold in half to wrong side and stitch in place.

Beginning at the underarm, bind the armholes with bias satin in this way, extending the border to form a strap 25cm/10in long, or required length for shoulder strap, folding the binding over on itself.

Join side seams. Round off the lower edge slightly and then hem.

5 cm

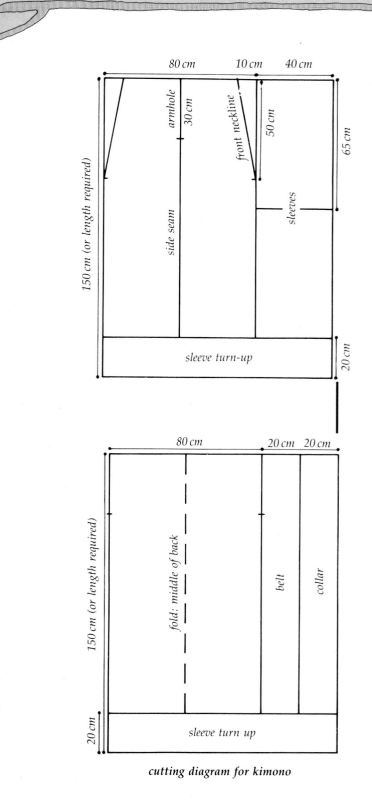

cutting diagram for kimono

(top diagram labels)
- 80 cm · 10 cm · 40 cm
- armhole
- 30 cm
- front neckline
- 50 cm
- 65 cm
- 150 cm (or length required)
- side seam
- sleeves
- sleeve turn-up
- 20 cm

(bottom diagram labels)
- 80 cm · 20 cm · 20 cm
- 150 cm (or length required)
- fold: middle of back
- belt
- collar
- 20 cm
- sleeve turn up

Kimono

This design is for the experienced needlewoman and the instructions do not include details for assembling the pieces. This model will fit up to 107cm/42in bust.

Materials

Fabric: 3m/3yd of 120cm/48in wide satin crepe for the background material; 0.75m/¾yd of 120cm/48in wide satin crepe for the applique motifs; synthetic padding material to use under the motifs.

Paints: use diluted grey for the background material; for the motifs, use all the colours in your palette, with one cockerel predominantly fiery red and the other jade green.

Gutta: grey.

Method examples

Work on the garment and the applique motifs separately. Use the matt side of the silk for the garment and the shiny side for the motifs. Prepare a large quantity of grey for the background and apply evenly. Cut out the pieces as given in the diagram.

To work the motifs, apply the gutta thickly over the outlines of the design as the satin crepe absorbs a lot of paint. Take great care with painting, as the crepe has a tendency to stretch.

To make up

Assemble the kimono. Make a wide tie belt to required length.

Place the padding under the motifs, cut round the contours and position them on the kimono.

Stitch the motifs in place with a tight zigzag stitch, sewing round the outer edges of the motifs. Sew over the gutta lines with straight stitch.

Brightly coloured cockerels enliven the simple shape of the wrap-over kimono. The motifs are worked separately and then padded and sewn on to the background.

chart for bird motifs on kimono

6 cm

Chemise and knicker set

This set is to fit an 86cm/34in bust and 91cm/36in hips.

Materials

Fabric: silk brocade with a small, self-coloured pattern. This pattern determines the silk design as the contours of the brocade are surrounded in gutta.

The chemise uses a length of about 91cm/36in by 48cm/19in wide.

The knickers use about 60cm/24in by 51cm/20in.

Narrow lace for trimming, if required.

Paints: scarlet, fuchsia, cobalt blue, duck egg blue, amethyst, chrome yellow and combinations of these colours as well as diluted versions.

Gutta: colourless.

Method examples

The design does not have to be drawn first. Outline the contours of the brocade patterns with gutta.

Paint each motif in colours as required using very diluted shades.

To make up

Cut the length for the chemise in half, one piece each for the back and front. Take sufficient off the length of each piece to make the shoulder straps.

Round the corners of the lower edges. Join side seams. Hem top edge and sew on made-up straps. Hem lower edges and trim with lace.

Cut out the knickers from the diagram given on page 36. Join centre front and back seams. Insert gusset.

Join side seams. Hem top edge and thread with elastic. Hem lower edges and trim with lace.

Pretty as a picture in a simple chemise and matching knickers. You can omit the lace trimmings, or be lavish and edge the top of the chemise as well.

Camisole and knicker set

The camisole size is adjustable; the knickers fit 91cm/36in hips.

Materials

Fabric: allow a total of approximately 1.5m/1½yd of silk crepe.

Paints: ruby red, pink, amethyst, jade, cobalt blue, black, lemon yellow and combinations of these colours as well as diluted versions.

Gutta: pink

Method examples

The crepe will be easier to handle if you wet the surface before painting. Use all the colours very diluted. For the foliage use water and alcohol mixed with jade and yellow.

To make up

Cut out the knickers from the diagram, allowing 2cm/¾in extra at the top for hem. Join centre front and back seams. Join the two pieces for the gusset and insert. Join side seams. Hem top edge and thread with elastic. Either scallop the lower edges with machine stitching or hem.

Cut the camisole front with a V-neck as shown in the illustration, having a side seam length of about 45cm/18in. Cut the back with a straight neck edge. Use the remaining fabric for shoulder straps, (or use toning ribbon), and bias edging for the neck, if required.

Join side seams. Either scallop the top edge with machine stitching or add a bias border. Hem lower edge. Sew on shoulder straps.

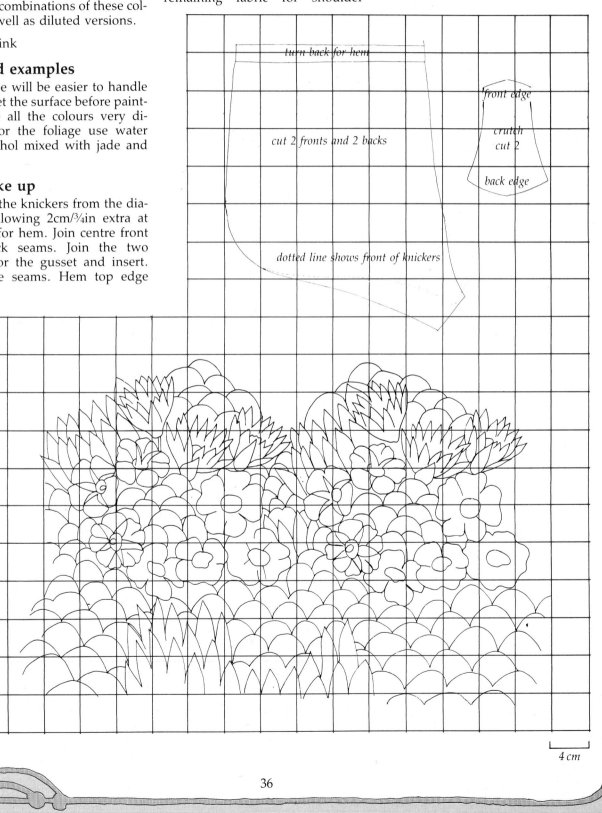

4 cm

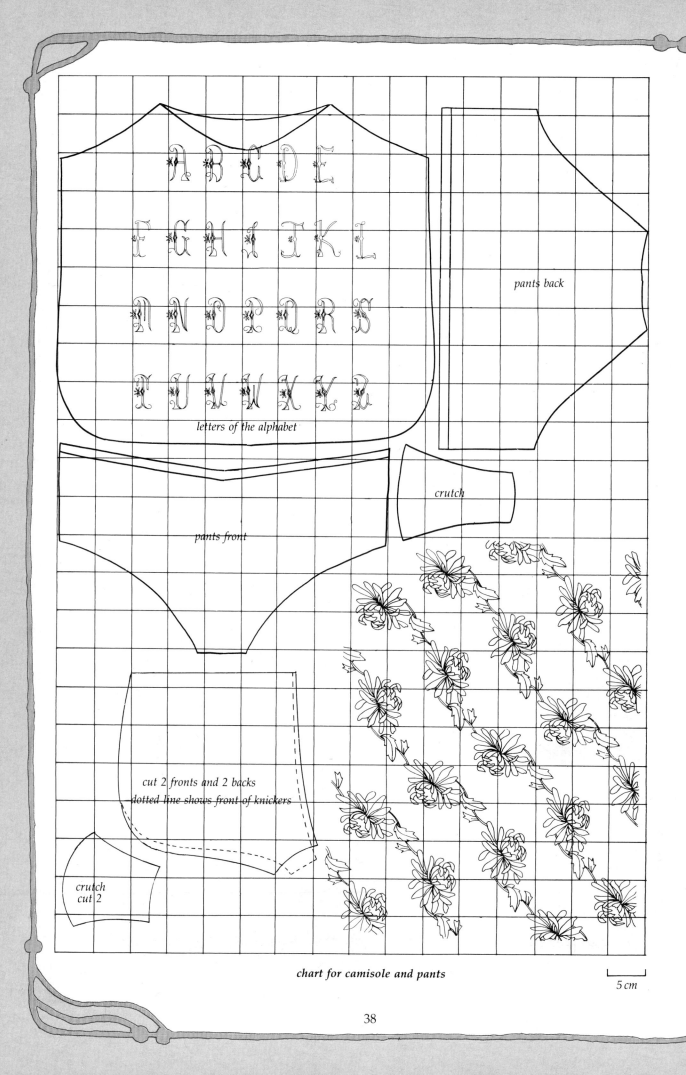

letters of the alphabet

pants back

pants front

crutch

cut 2 fronts and 2 backs
dotted line shows front of knickers

crutch
cut 2

chart for camisole and pants

5 cm

Flowered lingerie

The chemise and camisole shown here can be made to any size; the pants and knickers fit 91cm/36in hips.

Materials

Fabric: silk crepe, for the chemise and camisole allow about a total length of 91cm/36in and the width required to fit bust size; for the pants and knickers allow a total length of 91cm/36in; lace trimming if required.

Paints: pink, gold-yellow, jade, duck egg blue, ruby red and combinations of these colours as well as diluted versions.

Gutta: colourless tinted with a little yellow and a drop of red.

Method examples

Use all the colours diluted. Shade the petals in two tones of pink, mixing the pink with ruby red. Lighten them with a little yellow at the edges.

The leaves and stems are pale green, lightened with a little yellow or duck egg blue.

Use colours as required for the letters of the alphabet, to add your initials to the camisole.

To make up

Cut the knickers from the diagram and assemble as given on page 36. Cut the pants from the diagram. Insert gusset. Join side seams. Hem top edge and thread with elastic. Hem lower edges and trim with lace.

Cut the back and front for the chemise. Join side seams, leaving a slit of 10cm/4in at each side. Hem top edge and sew on straps, making 2 small darts on front, level with straps. Hem lower edge.

Cut the back and front of the camisole and assemble as given on page 36.

Silk tops and blouses

Summer tops and blouses in hand-painted silk make even the most ordinary outfit look special. They can be teamed with anything from a toning silk skirt to a pair of denim jeans. As with any hand-made garment, however, careful finishing is required if they are not to appear 'home-made'.

With the exception of a simple chemise shape, tops and blouses must either make provision for a neck opening so that the garment can be pulled on over the head, or button and buttonhole fastenings on the back or front. For a high boat-shaped neck, a very effective method is to complete the neckline with knitted ribbing, matching this finish on the armholes. For deep boat-shaped, or V-shaped styles, the neckline must be faced with matching fabric. On a buttoned garment, it is the neatness of the buttonholes which will make or mar the design.

Knitted edges

The silk fabric and the knitting yarn must be of similar weights. If the yarn is too heavy it will pull the silk out of shape; cotton yarn will give the best results.

Cast on a number of stitches which will give the required length of single ribbing to go round the opening, without stretching the knitting. Work 8 or more rows of ribbing, depending on the depth of band required, then cast off very loosely; use one size larger needle than recommended for the yarn to cast off the stitches.

With the right sides facing each other, sew the cast-off edge of the knitting to the silk, using back stitch, gently easing the knitting into position.

Back stitch: this method is worked by hand. With the right sides of both pieces facing each other, place the knitted edging on top of the silk. Sew along the wrong side of the knitted edge about 6mm/¼in from the edge, or just below the row of cast-off stitches. Secure a length of sewing yarn at the right-hand edge of the seam with a few running stitches and sew from right to left along the seam.
* With the needle at the back of the silk, move along to the left the width of one knitted stitch and push the needle through both pieces to the front, then pull the thread through.

Pass the needle across the front of the knitting from left to right and push it through both pieces at the end of the last stitch from the front to the back, (see Fig a).

Continue in this way from the asterisk, *, until the seam is completed, gently easing in the knitting. Do *not* stretch the knitting, or the silk fabric will pucker. Fasten off with a few small running stitches.

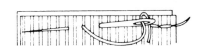

fig a   seaming ribbing to fabric

wrong side of ribbing

Faced edges

Before seaming the garment, cut a paper pattern of the shape of the edge which is to be faced, making an allowance of approximately 6.5cm/2½in for the depth of the facing. Cut out the facing from matching silk fabric.

Join the seams of the garment and the facing. Place the right sides of the edges of the garment and facing together and tack, then seam them, (see Fig b). Turn the garment right side out and tack along the faced edge, then gently press the edge. Remove the tacking.

fig b

shows wrong side of facing and right side of main fabric

Neaten the remaining raw edge of the facing with a hem, either by hand or machine. Catch down the outer edge of the facing on the shoulder or side seams, (see Fig c).

fig c

neatening raw edges of facing

Buttonholes

Hand worked buttonholes give the best finish on a silk garment. Horizontal buttonholes should have one square end and a round end at the edge of the garment and vertical buttonholes need two square ends.

Before cutting the buttonhole, mark its position with a row of machine stitching through the edge of the garment, the facing and any interfacing. Make sure the

Above: For details of this striking top, see overleaf.

41

length will be sufficient to take the size of button. Cut along the machine line and neatly oversew the two cut edges.

With the right side of the work facing you, insert a threaded needle from the wrong side through the fabric at the end of the lower edge of the opening, about 3mm/ ⅛in below the cut. Work in buttonhole stitch along the lower edge of the cut, (see Fig d).

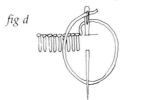

buttonhole stitching along lower edge

If the buttonhole has a rounded end, work approximately 9 whipping stitches, or the same number on a square end, then buttonhole stitch along the other edge of the cut. Complete with whipping stitches at the square end.

Top with knitted edges

This top fits an 86-91cm/34-36in bust very loosely; the size is adjustable.

Materials

Fabric: 2 lengths of silk satin to suit your requirements, approximately 64-66cm/25¼-26in wide; 2 × 50g balls of double knitting cotton; one pair 4mm/No 8 knitting needles.

Paints: scarlet, jade, chrome yellow, black and combinations of these colours as well as diluted versions.

Gutta: colourless.

Method examples

Buy the knitting cotton and then match the background colour to this. Use water and alcohol plus the colours required to match the yarn - we used scarlet and a little yellow.

Before painting the background, draw the design with gutta.

Flowers: Moisten the surface and paint the veins with quick brushstrokes using the same colour as the background, only a little more diluted. Add black shading.

Leaves: use very diluted jade green, lightened here and there with a little yellow.

To make up

Cut out the two pieces of silk. Join one shoulder seam. Tack side seams, leaving about 50-56cm/20-22in in all open for armholes, or depth required.

To knit the edges, cast on about 90 stitches, or number of stitches required for the back welt and work in single rib for the depth required, checking as you go that you have sufficient stitches. Cast off loosely. Work front welt in same way. Cast on about 118 stitches, or number required for each armband and work in same way. Cast on about 160 stitches, or number required for neckband and work in same way.

Neaten all raw edges. Machine the ribbing in place, with cast off edge to fabric, stretching to fit. Join remaining shoulder seam. Join side seams.

chart for top with knitted edges

4 cm

Flowered top

This top is simple to make from two rectangles of material, shaping the neckline slightly. The model shown here fits an 86–91cm/34–36in bust. The instructions do not include details for cutting or assembling the pieces. Beginners are advised to buy a suitable pattern.

Materials

Fabric: silk satin 61cm/24in wide by the length required, or according to your pattern.

Paints: pink, ruby red, chrome yellow, old gold, cobalt blue, black, duck egg blue, jade, Venetian red and combinations of these colours as well as diluted versions.

Gutta: pale pink.

Method examples

Draw the motifs and position them as shown in the illustration, then apply the gutta.

To paint the pink flowers, use mixtures of pink and ruby red, diluted as required. Add a few touches of pale green, (duck egg blue and very diluted chrome yellow), to some of the petals. Paint the centres with Venetian red, shaded with black.

To paint the green flowers, use different tones of green, tinted with varying amounts of yellow and blue, diluted as required. Add strokes of pink, cobalt blue or mauve, (pink and diluted cobalt blue). Paint the centres in ruby red or old gold, shaded with black.

The leaves surrounding the flowers range from pale grey-green to jade, darkened with black.

Paint the background with pure cobalt blue.

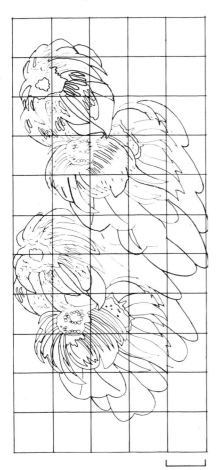

6 cm

43

Top with 'Bird of Paradise' motif

This simple top is decorated with the beautiful 'Bird of Paradise' bloom. The instructions do not include details for cutting out or assembling the pieces and beginners are advised to buy a suitable pattern.

You can use the small diagram to make a scarf, if you prefer.

Materials

Fabric: silk satin 61cm/24in wide by the length required, or according to your pattern.

Paints: scarlet, rust, tangerine, chrome yellow, golden-yellow, jade, duck egg blue, black, cobalt blue, azure blue, amethyst, navy blue and combinations of these colours as well as diluted versions.

Gutta: colourless.

Method examples

Draw the design and apply the gutta. Leave the background white.

For the flower use rust at the base of the petals, followed by scarlet, then tangerine, finishing with chrome yellow at the tip. Use tones of blue and amethyst to shade the blue parts of the flower.

Shade the leaves with dark green, (jade or duck egg blue and black), and yellow.

charts for 'Bird of Paradise' blouse and scarf

5 cm

Bold, bright colours are used for this beautiful flower motif, set against a plain white background. Use the instructions given on page 8 as the basis for a matching scarf.

Multi-floral top

Another simple shape which can be made from two rectangles of material, with a cut-out neckline. The instructions do not include details for cutting out or assembling the pieces.

Materials

Fabric: silk satin about 61cm/24in wide by the length required.

Paints: pink, fuchsia, tangerine, chrome yellow, jade, cobalt blue and combinations of these colours as well as diluted versions.

Gutta: colourless.

Method examples

Draw out the design, noting that only the pink flowers are shaded towards their centres. Leave the background white.

Opposite A riot of blossoms in strong colours highlight this simple shape.

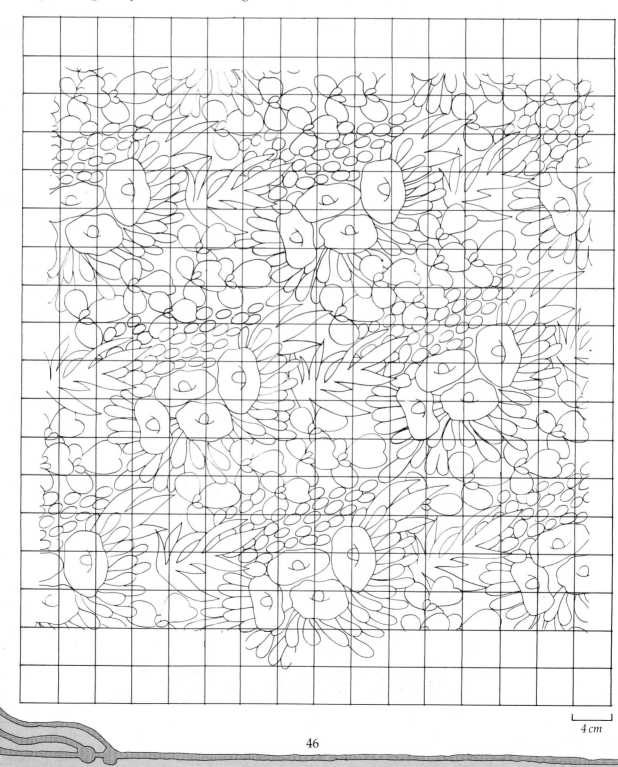

4 cm

Shirt blouse

This design is for the experienced needlewoman and the instructions do not include details for cutting out or assembling the pieces. This model fits an 86-91cm/34-36in bust size.

Materials

Fabric: silk crepe, allowing one piece 60cm/23½in by 80cm/31½in long for back; 2 pieces 42cm/16½in wide by 80cm/31½in for the fronts; 2 lengths 42cm/16½in wide by required length for sleeves; allow extra for facings, cuffs and all seams; buttons as required.

Paints: scarlet, azure blue, cobalt blue, navy blue, black, rosewood, leaf green, duck egg blue, jade, tangerine, yellow gold and combinations of these colours as well as diluted versions.

Gutta: green, pink, yellow.

Method examples

Match the colour of the gutta to the shapes you are going to outline. The background is scarlet, applied pure.

Wisteria: paint in a range of blues, used pure or diluted.

Lilies: leave almost white. Shade with very diluted pale grey, leaf green, pink and yellow.

Pink blooms: use diluted scarlet toned down with rosewood and grey shades, also very diluted.

Foliage: use predominantly blue and grey-green tones.

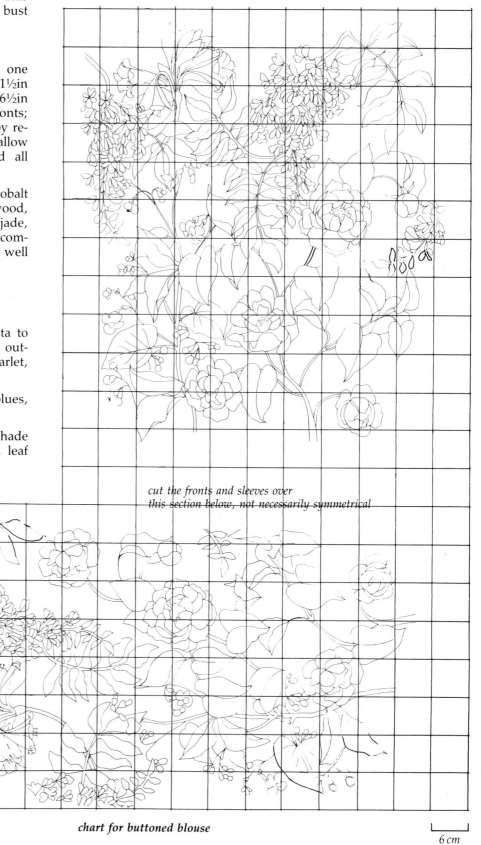

cut the fronts and sleeves over this section below, not necessarily symmetrical

chart for buttoned blouse

6 cm

Bathing belle

This shape is also easy to make from two rectangles of material, making provision for a V-neckline. The instructions do not include details for cutting or assembling the pieces. This model fits an 86-91cm/34-36in bust size.

Materials

Fabric: silk twill about 66cm/26in wide by the length required; bias borders for neckline and armholes.

Paints: carmine red, rosewood, yellow, azure blue, jade, navy blue, black and combinations of these colours as well as diluted versions.

Gutta: blue, pale yellow for diver's body.

Method examples

For the front, paint the diver's body with a mixture of rosewood, carmine red, yellow and water and alcohol. For the panel of blue sky, use azure blue with a little yellow and water and alcohol. The bright jade is slightly tinted with blue and applied diluted.

For the back, omit the figure of the diver.

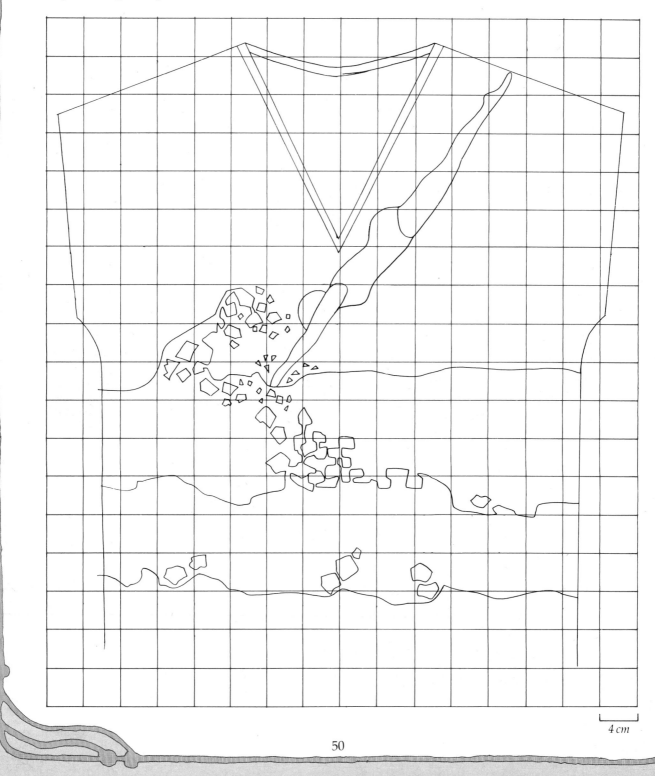

4 cm

The face of fashion

The shape of this design is as given for the Bathing belle shown on the previous page.

Materials

Fabric: silk twill about 73cm/29in wide by the length required; bias borders for neckline and armholes.

Paints: scarlet, tangerine, rosewood, yellow, dark brown, old gold, black, rust and combinations of these colours as well as diluted versions.

Gutta: black.

Method examples

Choose a different tone of beige or dark brown for each section of the background. Blend the rosewood and dark brown with old gold or scarlet, used pure or diluted.

Paint the face and neck with a mixture of rosewood, scarlet, yellow and water and alcohol.

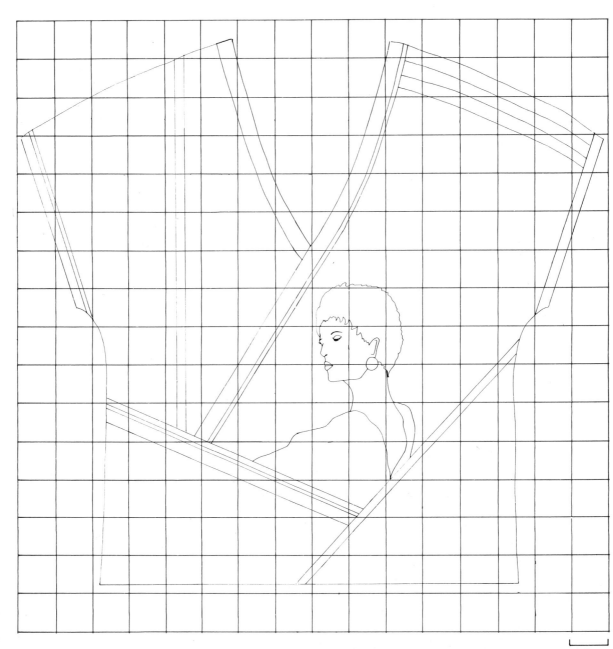

4.5 cm

Opposite: The clever use of painted diagonal lines on this blouse gives a crossover effect. The striking motif can be omitted, if you prefer.

Pink camisole top

This model fits an 86-91cm/34-36in bust size but the pattern can be adjusted to fit any size.

Materials

Fabric: silk crepe 51cm/20in wide, or half the required bust size plus 5cm/2in for ease of movement by the length required; satin bias for edges.

Paints: pink, fuchsia, black, chrome yellow, leaf green and combinations of these colours as well as diluted versions.

Gutta: colourless, black.

Method examples

Draw the design with gutta. The background is pink with a drop of slightly diluted fuchsia.

Leave some sections of the motifs white, paint others black and the remainder with chrome yellow and a little leaf green.

To make up

Join side seams. Sew on bias border to front and back neckline. Beginning at the underarm, sew on bias border to armholes, allowing about 25cm/10in for shoulder straps. Hem lower edge.

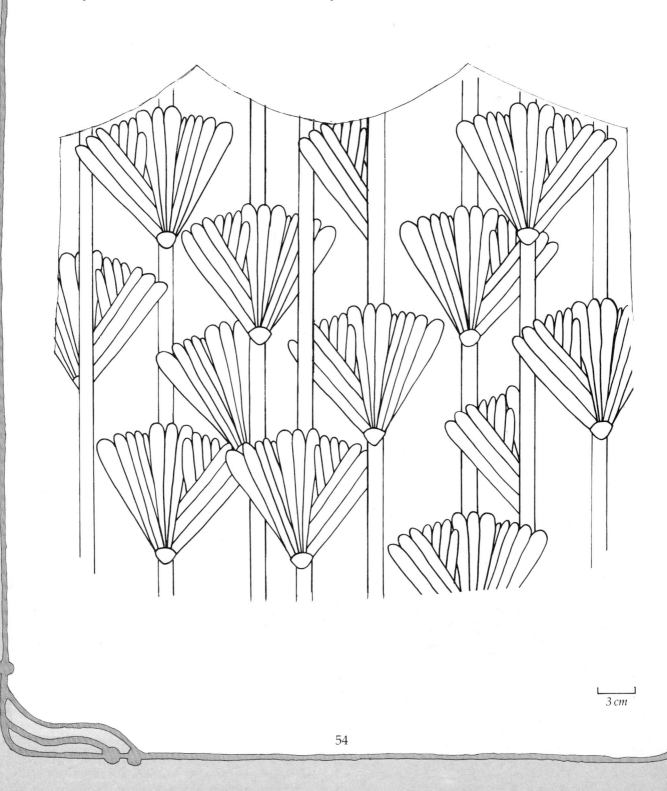

3 cm

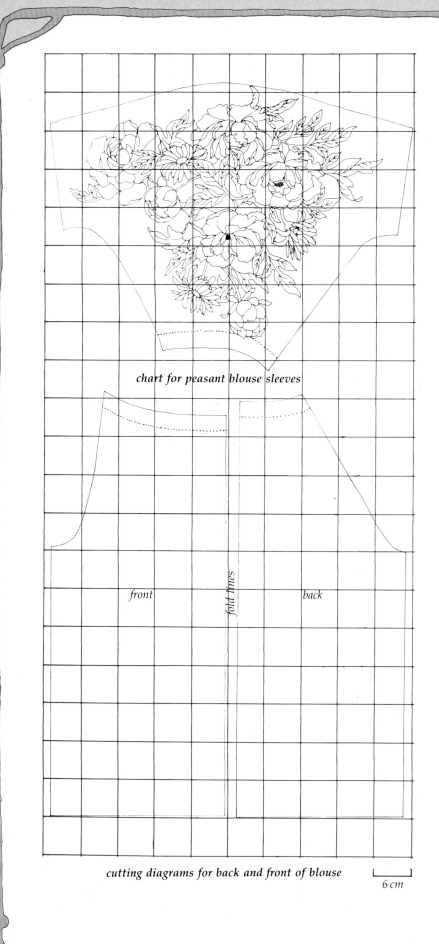

chart for peasant blouse sleeves

front

fold lines

back

cutting diagrams for back and front of blouse

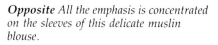

6 cm

Peasant blouse

The full sleeves of this dainty blouse are painted with blossoms. This model fits an 86-91cm/34-36in bust size but the pattern can be adjusted to fit any size.

Materials

Fabric: silk mousseline, (muslin), 112cm/44in wide by 140cm/55in long; fine cord and elastic.

Paints: scarlet, carmine red, navy blue, duck egg blue, rust, leaf green, rosewood and combinations of these colours.

Gutta: pale grey.

Method examples

The flowers are painted in pure colours. Using only a little colour on the brush, begin at the bottom of each petal, rinse the brush in water and smooth the paint while it is still wet towards the areas to be darkened. Rinse the brush well and then smooth towards the areas to be lightened.

To make up

Use French seams. Join the back and front and insert the sleeves.

Cut an opening at the centre front about 15cm/6in long and neatly hem this and lower edge of blouse. Place a bias edging round the neckline to form a casing. Insert a length of fine cord to tie at centre front. Hem the sleeves, inserting elastic.

Opposite All the emphasis is concentrated on the sleeves of this delicate muslin blouse.

Sleeveless top with large flowers

Two versions of this design are shown here, one white with pastel flowers, the other brown with bold flowers. The instructions do not include details for cutting or assembling the pieces. Both models fit an 86-91cm/34-36in bust size.

Materials

Fabric: silk twill about 51cm/20in wide by the length required.

Paints: for the white version, ruby red, yellow-gold, amethyst, jade; for the brown version, pink, ruby red, wine red, azure blue, navy blue, duck egg blue, rosewood, old gold.

Combinations of these colours for both versions as well as diluted colours.

Gutta: for the white version, pink; for the brown version, pink, clear blue.

Method examples

For the white version, use the colours very diluted. The shading is delicate and it will be easier if you wet each area with water before painting.

For the brown version, use pink gutta for the flowers and blue for the foliage. To leave white patches on the surface of the petals, cover each flower with antifixing solution after applying the gutta. This will still enable you to shade the inside of each petal. For the background, use rosewood, old gold and ruby red, all diluted.

Opposite: A sleeveless top decorated with huge blossoms.
Below: The same design worked in bright colours.

5 cm

Silk designs for children and babies

Every female, whatever her age, will appreciate the softness of silk. As it is a natural fibre, it is also wonderfully cool to wear in summer and surprisingly warm in winter. Add a glowing painted design to the silk and choose one of the designs given in this section to delight the heart of that very special little girl.

Pick a simple top for your first attempt and remember that you can add a knitted neck and armbands, see page 40 for instructions. If you don't feel confident enough to complete a dress, just use enough fabric to make a skirt and add an elastic waistband.

The skilled needlewoman can try her hand at quilting and add an extra dimension to the art of painting on silk.

Wadding

Quilting is a decorative way of stitching two or three layers of fabric together for additional warmth. In the designs shown here, the painted silk will be the top layer, followed by a layer of wadding and, finally, a plain silk lining. Most large stores and craft shops stock wadding made from man-made or natural fibres, available in different weights. For the designs in this section, pick a lightweight quality, as heavier weights will distort and pucker the silk. If you intend to hand-wash the garment, also make sure that the wadding is washable.

When cutting the wadding make sure that it is slightly larger than the area of the silk, as it will be reduced in size when it is stitched.

Hand quilting

It is easier to quilt the material before cutting out the separate pieces of a garment, as the fabric will lose some of its length and width due to the thickness of the wadding. It may help, however, to draw each pattern piece on the right side of the lining fabric as a guide.

Arrange the three layers of material with the lining at the bottom with the wrong side facing the wadding, then place the painted silk on the top with the wrong side facing the wadding. Tack all three pieces together, (see Fig a). When quilting by hand, use plenty of tacking stitches to ensure that the layers of material do not move.

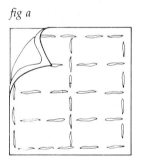

fig a

tacking 3 pieces together

A complex quilting design will need a template cut from cardboard or stiff paper but for straight vertical lines, or diamond shapes, mark the lines on white tissue or tracing paper at equal distances from each other. You may need several sheets to cover a large area.

Place the paper on top of the painted silk and pin or tack it in place. Using a fine needle and suitable sewing thread for the fabric, work along the lines with back stitch, or running stitch. Each stitch must be made in two separate movements; upwards and downwards through all three layers of material, (see Fig b). If the stitches are made in one movement they will not penetrate the wadding, so will not grip, allowing the materials to move. The length of each stitch must be governed by the thickness of the wadding. The paper can be eased away from the fabric as each line is completed.

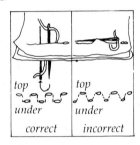

fig b

left-hand illustration shows correct method of working running stitches

Machine quilting

Arrange the layers of fabric as given for hand quilting but just lightly tack them together. For a complex quilting design draw it out on tracing paper and pin, or tack, the paper to the top layer of the material. As you stitch through the paper, tear it away.

For straight lines, however, most sewing machines are supplied with a distance piece which will enable you to work parallel lines at equal distances apart. When working diamond shapes or squares, machine stitch the lines in one direction first. Before going back to work the lines in the other direction, fluff up the wadding with a fine needle.

Always push the fabric gently through the machine; do not pull it through as this will flatten the wadding.

Opposite: Machine-quilt this attractive jacket for extra warmth. See overleaf for chart and instructions.

Child's quilted jacket

This design is for an experienced needlewoman and the instructions do not include details for assembling or finishing off the pieces. This model fits a six year old.

Materials

Fabric: silk twill 50cm/19¾in wide by 60cm/23½in long to fit the size of fabric design; allow 2 lengths for the jacket body and 2 lengths for the sleeves; lining fabric and satin bias for edges; padding.

Paints: ruby red, rust, duck egg blue, old gold, chrome yellow, black, pink and combinations of these colours as well as diluted versions.

Gutta: yellow.

Method examples

Use ruby red mixed with rust for the background.

Shade the flowers, animals and figures as illustrated, sometimes applying the paints pure and at other times diluting them.

Note

The fabric design we suggest has been adapted to fit the pattern for the jacket shown on the previous page. This can be reduced or enlarged to fit a pattern suitable for your own requirements.

collar

5 cm

dotted lines show front pattern

sleeves

fronts and back

foldline of back and front

chart for girl's quilted jacket

5 cm

Child's T-shirt

This design is easy to make from two rectangles of material, shaping the neckline slightly. The instructions do not include details for cutting or assembling the pieces. This model fits a six-to-eight year old.

Materials

Fabric: silk crepe about 41cm/16in wide by the length required, or according to your pattern.

Paints: scarlet, chrome yellow, azure blue, duck egg blue, rosewood, pink and combinations of these colours as well as diluted versions.

Gutta: vermilion red, yellow, black, grey.

Method examples

Match the colour of the gutta to the area to be surrounded. Use grey gutta for the waves and cloud.

Shade the bodies in tones of rosewood, used diluted. On the thighs, stomach and pale parts of the arms, push the colour back,

using a brush dipped in pure alcohol. Put a little diluted pink on the cheeks while still wet.

Paint the sea in azure and duck egg blue, applied pure. The sky is azure blue very diluted.

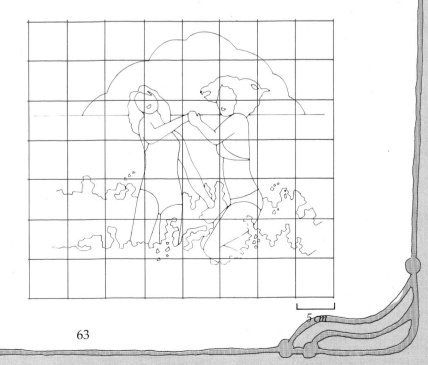

5 cm

Child's skirt and top

A dandy lion chases butterflies on this charming design! It can be made to fit any size.

Materials

Fabric: pongé No 10; for the skirt measure the length required, then add 6cm/2¼in for the hem and the same amount for the elasticated waistband, allowing a width of two-and-a-half times the waist size; for the top measure the shoulder width, adding a further 5cm/2in for ease of movement and 4cm/1½in for seams, by the length required, allowing 10cm/4in for hem and seam allowance, then cut two rectangles for the front and back shaping the neckline as shown.

Paints: scarlet, yellow-gold, old gold, leaf green, dark brown and combinations of these colours as well as diluted versions.

Gutta: pale yellow.

Method examples

Reproduce the pattern on the skirt with two lions facing each other, plus one butterfly and one cactus, as shown. Draw one complete motif on the front of the top.

Add a few strokes of old gold and dark brown to the mane. The stripes on the mane are scarlet, mixed with yellow-gold and leaf green, all used very diluted.

To make up

Join the back seam of the skirt, leaving an opening of about 10cm/4in, then baste the sides of the opening. Make a double waistband for the elastic, thread the elastic through and close the end. Hem lower edge. Fasten waistband with hook and eye.

Join the shoulders of the top. Join side seams leaving enough open for the armholes. Bind the neckline and armholes with bias borders. Hem lower edge.

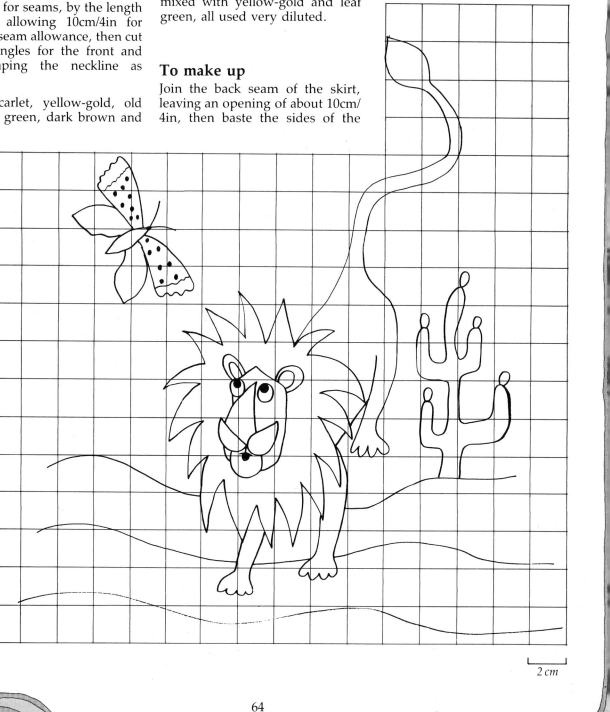

2 cm

Above: *Friendly lions frolic all over this cool summer top and skirt.*

Child's flowered dress

Pastel flowers are scattered over this simple sun-dress. It can be made to fit any size.

Materials

Fabric: silk twill; allow sufficient material for the yoke, which should come high enough to cover the chest at underarm level, the width equal to the chest measurement, plus 4cm/1½in extra for ease of movement and 4cm/1½in for seams, and two straps about 4cm/1½in wide.

For the skirt, measure the length required plus hem and allow two-and-a-half times the chest measurement for the width; zip fastener.

Paints: pink, fuchsia, amethyst, chrome yellow, tangerine, azure blue, Prussian blue, duck egg blue, jade and combinations of these colours as well as diluted versions.

Gutta: pink.

Method examples

Reproduce the pattern as many times as necessary across the width of the skirt, one time facing upwards and the next downwards, as indicated by the dotted line on the chart. Choose some of the flowers to scatter across the yoke. Use all the colours diluted; there is no shading.

To make up

Fold the yoke so that two short ends are at centre back. Seam the straps and sew in place to top of yoke at front and back.

Join the skirt seam to form centre back, leaving an opening of about 10-15cm/4-6in. Gather up the top edge of the skirt to fit along the lower edge of yoke and stitch in place.

Sew in zip fastener to centre back seam, to come to top of yoke.

Opposite: Pretty as a picture in this delicately patterned sun dress.

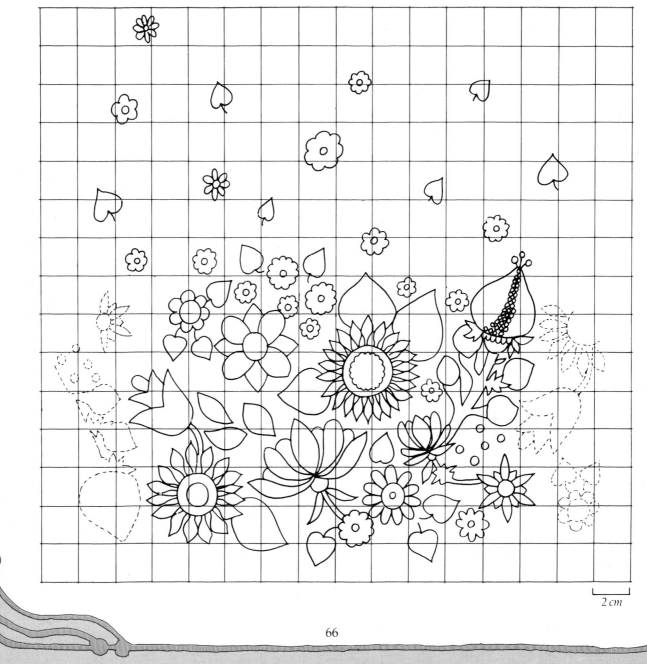

2 cm

Child's top with knitted edge

You can make this top to any size by cutting two rectangles of material, shaping the neckline to the required depth and adding a knitted welt.

Materials

Fabric: silk satin, to measurements required; 1 × 50gm ball of double knitting cotton to match the background colour of the silk.

Paints: vermilion, fuchsia, yellow-gold, turquoise, jade, rosewood and combinations of these colours as well as diluted versions.

Gutta: colourless.

Method examples

Use water and alcohol plus vermilion and rosewood for the body. Dilute the colours for the icecream cone, the leotard and the skirt.

For the background, use yellow-gold plus a little vermilion.

To make up

Join shoulder seams. Join side seams leaving enough open for the armholes. Neaten neck and armhole edges.

Cast on sufficient stitches with 4mm/No 8 needles to go right round lower edge.

Work in single rib for required depth of welt. Cast off loosely. Sew in place with cast off edge to fabric, stretching to fit. Join seam.

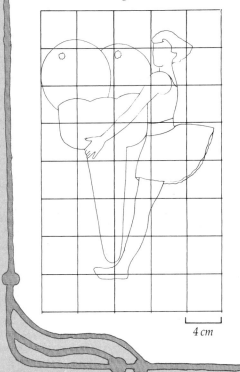

4 cm

Child's top with pelican motif

Pick a pelican for this simple summer top - you can make it to any size by cutting two rectangles of material and shaping the neckline to the required depth.

5 cm

Materials

Fabric: silk satin to measurements required.

Paints: ruby red, pink, amethyst, chrome yellow, tangerine, jade, duck egg blue, azure blue and combinations of these colours as well as diluted versions.

Gutta: colourless.

Method examples

For the background use water and alcohol plus duck egg blue and azure blue.

Keep the pelican white, with pinky-beige shading, (pink plus a dash of yellow).

For the water in the pool use diluted amethyst.

Shade the sun with colours ranging from diluted pink to diluted tangerine. Use pure jade for the palms.

For the ground use very diluted green-yellow and shade with pale pink.

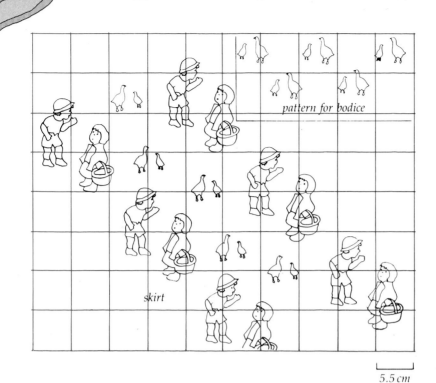

5.5 cm

Child's sun-dress

This design can be made to fit any size.

Materials

Fabric: silk twill, see Child's flowered dress on page 66 for amount.

Paints: scarlet, chrome yellow, azure blue, duck egg blue, black, tangerine, yellow-gold and combinations of these colours as well as diluted versions.

Gutta: yellow, black.

Method examples

Repeat the pattern all over the surface of the material, using the geese only for the bodice.

The colours are applied flat, either pure or slightly diluted. Add touches of pink to the cheeks whilst they are still wet.

To make up

See instructions for Flowered dress on page 66, but form the shoulder straps into bows.

Opposite: This sleeveless jacket for a baby is quilted and edged with fur. Instructions are also given for making the matching bootees. See overleaf for charts and details.

Baby boutique

This little sleeveless jacket and matching bootees would make the ideal gift for the latest female in the family. The jacket fits a 56cm/22in chest size, (about 9 months old), and the soles of the bootees measure 10cm/4in long.

Materials

Fabric: pongé No 10 cut to the size shown in the pattern; cotton for lining; padding; synthetic fur for the jacket, if required; about 20cm/7¾in by 40cm/15¾in white felt for the bootees, and ribbon, 6mm/¼in wide.

Paints: leaf green, royal blue, chrome yellow, pink, amethyst and combinations of these colours as well as diluted versions.

Gutta: pale green, (green and yellow), colourless.

Method examples

Cut the jacket in one piece and reproduce the design symmetrically on either side of the centre back fold.

Draw the leaves and stalks with green gutta and the flowers with colourless gutta. Shade the foliage in tones ranging from leaf green to a mixture of leaf green and royal blue, or leaf green and yellow. The colour of the flowers should range from pink to amethyst.

To make up

Jacket: place a layer of padding on the reverse side of the painted silk. Cut the lining to the size of the jacket and draw a grid on the right side of about 4cm/1½in diamond shapes. Place on top of the padding and stitch along the grid lines. Join shoulder seams. Sew round the outer edge and armholes, inserting the fur into all the seams.

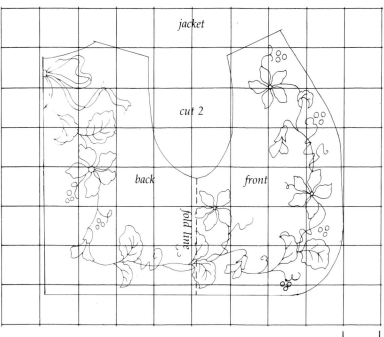

4 cm

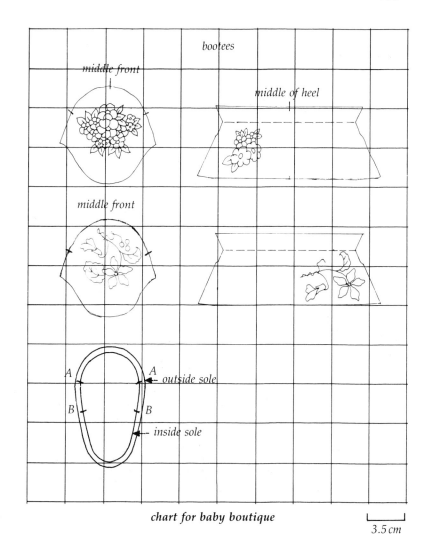

chart for baby boutique

3.5 cm

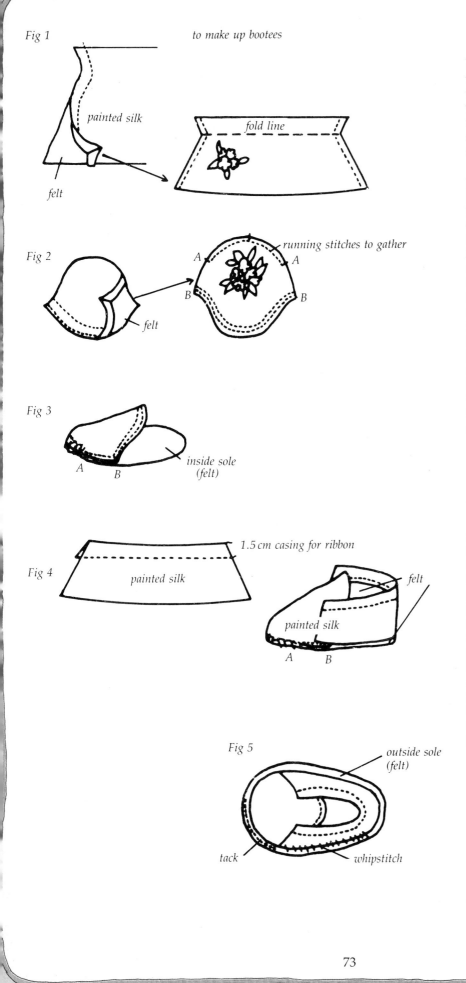

Fig 1

to make up bootees

painted silk

felt

fold line

Fig 2

running stitches to gather

A   A

B   B

felt

Fig 3

A   B

inside sole
(felt)

Fig 4

1.5 cm casing for ribbon

painted silk

felt

painted silk

A   B

Fig 5

outside sole
(felt)

tack   whipstitch

Bootees: cut out the painted silk to the pattern, allowing 2cm/¾in for the seams. Cut the felt inner lining without an allowance and the inner sole using the inside contour shown in the pattern and the outer sole using the outside contour.

For the heel section fold and press the silk along its top edge, (Fig 1), and place on the corresponding piece of felt; make 2 rows of top stitches one 6mm/¼in from the side edge, the other about 2mm/⅛in from the other side edge as shown. Work the foot front in the same way as shown, (Fig 2), then gather up between the 2 marks A to A. Fold lower edge to the inside, pin the inner sole to the foot front, lining up A to A, and B to B, and stitch between these marks on the right side of the fabric, through all layers, 2mm/⅛in from the edge. Secure the foot front between A to A by hand using whipstitch, (Fig 3).

Complete the heel, (Fig 4), by sewing along the top edge for the casing 2mm/⅛in from the edge. Fold the lower edge in and position the heel on the inner sole, making sure it is central. Sew on the right side about 2mm/⅛in from the edge through all layers. Place the bootee on the outer sole and secure with a little adhesive to hold it in place, tack all round the edge. Fold in the heel edge and sew in place with buttonhole thread, using whipstitch. Thread the ribbon through the casing to tie at front.

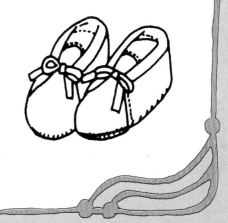

Silk holiday wear

Silk is the ideal fabric for hot summer days, as it hangs beautifully without clinging to the body. This section features simple shift dresses and elegant pareos, which can be tied and draped in a variety of ways.

When painting large areas of fabric, it is essential to work swiftly. You must also ensure that you have mixed sufficient quantities of each colour to complete a project. When making a pareo, it may be best to keep to white or cream silk for the background, to avoid painting over very large areas. If you do use a pastel coloured silk, remember that you will not be able to introduce any white into the design.

Ways of tying a pareo

The word 'pareo' is Tahitian and it means a large, rectangular piece of flowered material, usually cotton.

On this page and the following two pages we have given some ideas on how to wear a pareo. It is the way in which it is tied that gives it such versatility - either loose and casual for the beach, or accessorised with a belt as a party piece!

We have given you just a few suggestions but if you experiment you are sure to discover new ways.

Method A
With the centre of the pareo level with the middle of your back, drape it round you from the back.

Fig 1: take the two ends and cross them at the front.

Fig 2: tie the ends at the back of the neck.
This is the classic way to tie a pareo.

Opposite: A pareo is the ideal beach wrap and can be worn in a variety of ways. See page 78 for charts and instructions.

◁ **Fig 1**: take the two ends, place the larger piece over the right shoulder and the smaller piece under your left arm.

Method B

With the centre of the pareo positioned slightly to the left of the middle of your back, drape it round you from the back.

Fig 2: tie at the back.

Fig 3: this makes a very attractive off the shoulder dress.

◁ **Fig 1**: tie at the front.

Method C

With the centre of the pareo level with the middle of your back, drape it round from the back.

Fig 2: take the ends round and tie at the centre back neck.

Fig 3: this method forms a halter neck with soft folds of silk at the front.

Method D

With the centre of the pareo positioned slightly to the left of the middle of your back, drape it round you from the back.

Method E

With the centre of the pareo level with your left underarm, drape it round you to the right side.

Fig 1: take hold of the pareo about 20cm/7¾in from each end.

Fig 2: tie in a bow at the side. This makes a pretty strapless dress.

Fig 1: tie the ends in a bow to give an asymmetric effect. This method can be cinched at the waist with a wide belt.

Method F

With the centre of the pareo level with the middle of your back, drape it round you from the back.

Fig 1: tie in a knot at the centre front. This is probably the most popular way of wearing a pareo.

6 cm

Butterfly pareo

This design fits any size, see page 75 for illustration.

Materials

Fabric: silk crepe, 190cm/75in long by 115cm/45in wide.

Paints: wine red, rust, leaf green, black, yellow-gold, old gold, tangerine, azure blue, navy blue, duck egg blue and combinations of these colours as well as diluted versions.

Gutta: yellow.

Method examples

For the green foliage use leaf green pure, leaf green with diluted yellow and varying amounts of duck egg blue.

For the red grasses use rust and wine red; the pointed tips are slightly tinted with black.

For the speckled parts of the butterflies' wings place small strokes of colour side by side. On the other bands paint blue or rust patches while the surface is still wet.

For the stripes at the lower edge, use rust, tangerine, slightly diluted leaf green and old gold.

charts for pareo

Flowered pareo

This design is extremely generous and will fit any size.

Materials

Fabric: silk crepe, 190cm/75in long by 120cm/48in wide.

Paints: yellow-gold, black, azure blue, Prussian blue, jade, duck egg blue and combinations of these colours.

Gutta: black.

Method examples

Repeat the pattern along the length of the fabric, arranging the flowers and leaves in bands and turning each new band in the opposite direction.

At the top and bottom of the fabric, draw 4 stripes 2cm/¾in, 2cm/¾in, 1cm/½in and 3cm/1¼in wide respectively.

The colours are applied flat; this will take some time but is not difficult. For the leaves use jade with a little yellow, duck egg blue and green and pure Prussian blue.

The background is pure yellow-gold.

5 cm

Beach outfit

This short, simple shift dress is the ideal beach cover-up. It is teamed with a matching beach bag.

The dress can be made to any size and instructions are not given for cutting the pattern. This model fits an 86-91cm/34-36in bust size.

Materials

Fabric: silk crepe, 2 lengths 91cm/36in wide for the dress; 55cm/21¾in square of the same for the bag, 2 wooden handles, clear stick-on plastic, 2 lengths of cord.

Paints: pink, fuchsia, azure blue, yellow-gold, old gold, rosewood, duck egg blue and combinations of these colours as well as diluted versions.

Gutta: black.

Method examples

On the dress, use rosewood with touches of pink and yellow, plus water and alcohol for the face. Add a touch of pink to the cheeks while they are still wet. Leave a few white trails in the sea to represent the waves. For the sky use water and alcohol with azure and duck egg blue.

On the bag, use the same design as for the dress, replacing the bather in the background with the smaller figure given in the chart. Paint as for the dress.

To make up

Dress: cut 2 rectangles to suit your measurements, shaping the neckline.

Join shoulder seams. Join side seams leaving required amount open for armholes. Bind neck and armholes with bias borders. Hem lower edge.

Bag: this can be lined with foam sponge if required. Seal the right side of the silk with stick-on clear plastic. Make hems at the top edges to take the handles. Attach the cord to the ends of each handle.

charts for dress and bag motifs

4 cm

Holiday dress

This cool shift dress is painted with Egyptian hieroglyphics. The instructions do not include details for cutting or assembling the pieces but you can use your own pattern. This model fits an 86-91cm/34-36in bust size.

Materials

Fabric: wild silk cut to suit your own measurements.

Paints: rust, yellow-gold, black and combinations of these colours.

Gutta: black.

Method examples

Paint over the entire surface of the fabric, repeating the motifs as required. Use dark grey for the motifs, leave some details white.

The background is orange, mixing rust and yellow-gold.

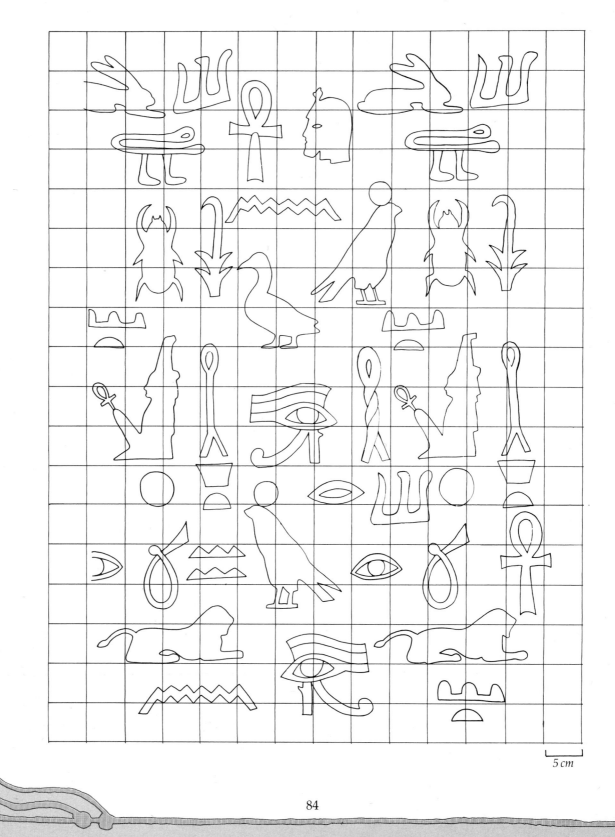

5 cm

84

Silk dresses and skirts

A pure silk, hand-painted dress or two-piece is the ideal choice for that special occasion. The painting can be as lavish as you like on a simple style but just add a delicate border on something as sumptuous as the wedding dress featured here.

When a dress has to be figure-fitting, rather than a loose shift style, it will need darts at such places as the bust, neck, waist and, maybe, shoulders. These darts take in any excess fullness and their position should be carefully marked on the fabric with tacking stitches. A bust dart should be placed level with the fullest part of the bust.

Where a garment cannot be pulled on over the head, such as a dress or skirt with a fixed waistband, it will also require a placket, closed with a zip fastener.

Darts

Sew the dart on the wrong side of the material by hand with small, back stitches, or by machine set at the correct tension for the fabric. Begin at the widest end of the dart and continue along to the point of the dart, (see Fig a). Do not stretch the dart as you stitch, as this will cause an ugly point on the right side of the garment.

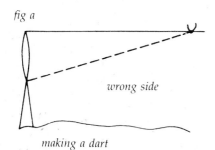

fig a

wrong side

making a dart

If sewing by hand, fasten off with two or three small running stitches, one on top of the other. To fasten off machine stitches, tie the two ends of thread together or darn them back into the machine stitches.

Plackets

Before inserting the zip fastener, make sure that it is suitable for silk fabric; an extra-lightweight quality is advised. Also check that it is to the correct length and on no account stretch the fabric when sewing in the zip, or it will buckle and not lie flat. Zip fasteners should be sewn in by machine, rather than by hand.

Straight seam: this is the easiest way of setting a zip into a dress or skirt, either on a side seam or centre back seam.

Begin by tacking along the seam line where the zip is to be inserted. With the wrong side of the fabric facing, place the centre of the zip on the seam line. Tack it in position along the turnings.

Turn the garment to the right side and with a zipper foot attached, sew about 6mm/¼in from the seam line, (see Figs b and c). Remove tacking.

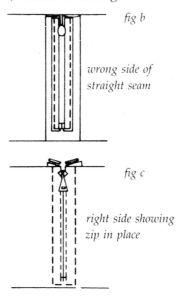

fig b

wrong side of straight seam

fig c

right side showing zip in place

To neaten the inside of the opening, oversew the raw edges of the fabric to the edges of the zip fastener.

Overlapped seam: this method conceals the zip when it is closed. Tack along the seam line as for a straight seam. Press the seam open and remove the tacking.

Tack the back edge of the seam close to the edge of the zip, extending the end of the seam by about 3mm/⅛in. Machine as close to the teeth of the zip as possible, allowing it to move freely, (see Fig d).

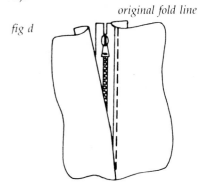

original fold line

fig d

With the front, overlapped edge of the seam touching the back edge of the opening, tack the other edge of the zip in place. Machine with the zipper foot about 6mm/¼in from the fold, (see Fig e).

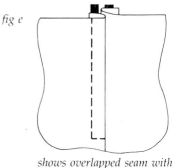

fig e

shows overlapped seam with zip in place

Work a bar across the bottom end of the zip where the two edges meet, with three or four back stitches (see Fig f). Neaten these with blanket stitches. Neaten the inside of the opening as for straight seam.

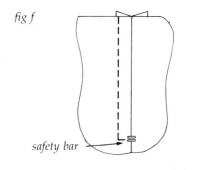

fig f

safety bar

Above: This romantic wedding dress is made from silk chiffon.
See overleaf for charts and instructions.

Wedding dress

This design is for an experienced dressmaker and the instructions do not include precise details of cutting out or assembling the pieces.

The simplicity of the shape, however, should enable most needlewomen to cut the pattern to suit their own requirements. This model fits an 86-91cm/34-36in bust size.

Materials

Fabric: silk mousseline, (muslin), with satin self-stripes along one edge, 385cm/152in long by 120cm/47¼in wide; 150cm/59in of silk satin for trimmings; 2 lengths of tulle to line the skirt; 2 lengths of pongé No 10, 55cm/21¾in wide, for the petticoat.

Paints: Parma violet, dark pink, moss green and combinations of these colours as well as diluted versions.

Gutta: very clear grey.

Method examples

Trace the motifs in gutta, lightly brushing the surface of the silk.

Paint in very diluted colours, while the surface is still wet, shading in stronger tones.

To make up

Cut and assemble the bodice and raglan sleeves. Cut a satin bias 3cm/1¼in wide and edge the neckline.

Line the skirt with tulle and gather the top on to a length of 3cm/1¼in wide elastic. For the belt, cut a satin band 18cm/7in wide to your waist measurement, allowing 5cm/2in extra to fasten. Cut a band 18cm/7in wide by 3m/3yd long for the bow. Line the belt and bow with interlining and seam. Stitch the finished bow to the end of the belt, to come at centre back of the waist.

To make the strapless petticoat, cut 2 rectangles of fabric, 55cm/21¾in wide and length as required. Finish with very narrow elastic at the top of the bodice and at the waist.

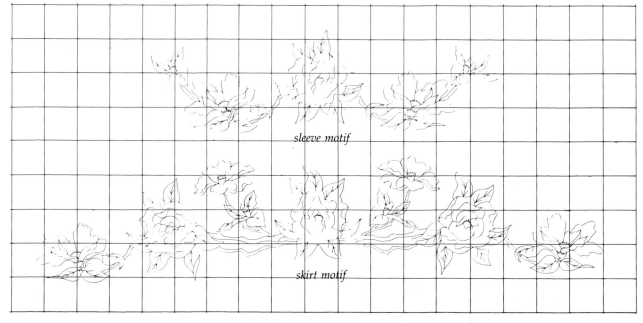

sleeve motif

skirt motif

chart for wedding dress

6 cm

Sundress

This design can be adapted to suit any size and the instructions do not include details for cutting out or assembling the pieces. This model fits an 86-91cm/34-36in bust size and 91-97cm/36-38in hips.

Materials

Fabric: silk crepe, 2 lengths about 91cm/36in long, cutting 2 pieces to fit the bodice size, 2 straps and 2 skirt sections.

Paints: scarlet, chrome yellow, yellow-gold, azure blue, Prussian blue, leaf green, tangerine and combinations of these colours as well as diluted versions.

Gutta: colourless, pale orange.

Method examples

The background colour is a slightly reddened tangerine, used very diluted. Prepare sufficient for all the fabric.

Don't expect to obtain good shading as the paint doesn't spread so freely on crepe. Vary the colours of the petals and leaves, starting with the brightest colour and working towards the palest, or white. Use a soft brush for the background.

We have given the drawing for half of the skirt width; reverse it for the second half. Reproduce the outer flowered band along the top edge of the bodice and on the straps.

Opposite: A riot of blossoms decorate this neat sleeveless top and matching skirt.

3.5 cm

Safari dress

This elegant dress can be adapted to suit any size and the instructions do not include precise details for cutting out the pieces. This model fits an 86-91cm/34-36in bust size and 91-97cm/36-38in hips.

Materials

Fabric: wild silk, 2 lengths about 240cm/94½in long by 91cm/36in wide, or to suit your own measurements.

Paints: wine red, yellow-gold, old gold, tangerine, black, leaf green, rosewood, dark brown and combinations of these colours as well as diluted versions.

Gutta: black.

Method examples

The background is a slightly diluted tangerine. Using brown, green, black, yellow, and wine red, paint the foliage in a range of tones. Shade the banana leaves lightly.

For the birds, paint patches of black, dark brown and leaf green on the yellow surface while still wet.

Paint the back of the dress in the same way as the front.

To make up

Mark the centre of the width of both the back and front. Cut out a neckline on the front about 8cm/3¼in deep and 25cm/9¾in wide. Shape the back neckline about 1cm/½in deep by 25cm/9¾in wide.

Join the shoulders. Make bust darts and join side seams. Edge the neckline and armholes with bias borders. Hem lower edge.

6.5 cm

Opposite: Tropical birds and foliage run riot on this sleeveless dress. It features neat bust darts.

Flowered top and skirt

This simple top and skirt can be adapted to suit any size. The instructions do not include precise details for cutting out the pieces. This model fits an 86-91cm/34-36in bust size and 91-97cm/36-38in hips.

Materials

Fabric: silk twill; for the skirt allow 2½ times your waist measurement for the width by the length required; for the top cut 2 rectangles about 55cm/21¾in wide by 65cm/25½in long, or to suit your own measurements.

Paints: pink, scarlet, tangerine, fuchsia, yellow-gold, navy blue, amethyst, rosewood and combinations of these colours as well as diluted versions.

Gutta: colourless.

Left: A simple summer top and matching skirt painted in a riot of colours.

Method examples

Reproduce the design in horizontal bands. Reverse the design each time, using the dotted lines on the right of the drawing as a guide. For the next band, reverse the design by turning the template and position it as indicated by the dotted lines shown on the lower edge of the drawing.

The flowers and leaves should be well shaded, allowing the orange to be fairly strong but keeping the other colours pale.

The background varies, using a mixture of pale duck egg blue, amethyst, (mixing these 2 colours gives grey), grey-greens or green tinted with yellow, applied in patches.

To make up

Top: mark the centre of the width of both rectangles and cut out a circular neckline, about 8cm/3¼in deep and 25cm/9¾in wide. Join shoulder seams. Join side seams, leaving about 24cm/9½in open for the armholes. Edge the neckline and armholes with bias borders. Hem the lower edge.

Skirt: join the centre back seam, leaving an opening of about 10cm/4in. Stitch the sides of this opening. Gather the waist edge and sew on a waistband, stiffened with grosgrain ribbon. Close with hooks and eyes. Hem the lower edge.

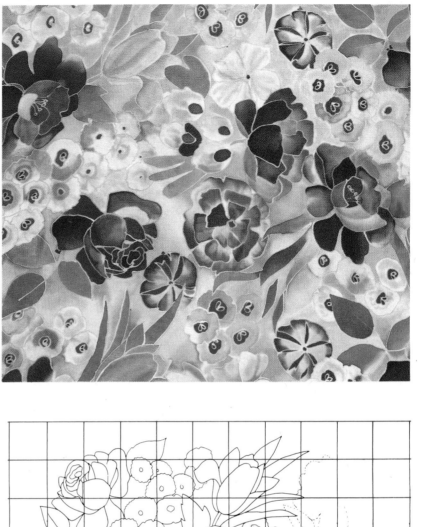

5 cm

Summer skirt and top

This design can be adapted to suit any size and the instructions do not include details of cutting out or assembling the pieces. Beginners should buy a pattern to suit their requirements. This model fits an 86-91cm/34-36in bust size and 91-97cm/36-38in hips.

Materials

Fabric: silk taffeta, about 145cm/57in by 91cm/36in for the skirt; 100cm/39½in by 60cm/23½in for the top.

Paints: brown, caramel, carmine red and combinations of these colours.

Gutta: colourless.

Method examples

If you are working from a dress-making pattern, check the measurements and prepare the pieces to be painted. Cut the silk large enough for the design and leave a wide margin round the edges. When the painting is completed, trim to the exact measurements of the pattern.

Alternate the brown and caramel to paint the leaf motifs. Apply the gutta as you work, so that you can leave white areas.

For the top, use brown for the background, sprinkle coarse salt over the surface while the paint is still wet.

5 cm

Silk jackets and pullovers

Once you have completed the silk painting for a garment, and prior to the final stages of assembling the sections, you can easily add further details, or define outlines with embroidery stitches and beading. In adding these embellishments, however, take care not to over-gild the lily!

You may find a painted area is not to your entire satisfaction; why not cover it up with simple embroidery stitches? These will look best worked in stranded embroidery silk, to complement the silk fabric. Alternatively, you may discover an error in the painting which cannot be corrected; cover it with a few sequins or tiny beads and no-one will be the wiser!

The designs featured in this section use added embroidery, beads, applique, as well as simple quilting to very great effect. They are intended for the skilled needlewoman, who also has some knowledge of these techniques.

Simple embroidery stitches

The stitches shown here are probably familiar to most embroiderers and can be used in many different ways. They can all be worked freehand, without the aid of a transfer but take care to keep the stitches regular and even, (see Fig a).

Simple beading techniques

Beads can be obtained from craft stores and come in a variety of different sizes, materials and shapes, and all the colours of the rainbow.

The shapes include smooth and faceted round versions, smooth and faceted cylindrical and smooth and faceted drops. Those made from glass or plastic are the most suitable for applying to silk. Glass beads reflect the light better and will add a shimmer to the silk but plastic beads are lighter in weight and will not pull the fabric out of shape. All versions have a central hole.

Unless the beads you are using have large holes, you will need a special fine beading needle to slip them on to the thread, ready to apply to the silk. Use spun nylon thread or ordinary sewing thread to stitch the beads in place.

To apply beads singly, tie a knot in the thread and push the needle through the fabric from the wrong side. Pull the thread through. Slip the bead on to the needle and down the thread, level with the surface of the fabric. Push the needle through the fabric to the wrong side to secure the bead and either fasten off securely, or continue placing the beads in position as required, (see Fig b).

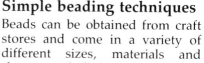

fig b

applying a single bead

To apply beads in groups, tie a knot in the thread and push the needle through the fabric from the wrong side. Pull the thread through. Slip the number of beads required on to the needle and down the thread, level with the surface of the fabric, then push the needle through to the wrong side of the fabric. Bring the needle up again in position as required and continue placing strings of beads, (see Fig c).

fig c

small beads

large beads

working a flower with strings of beads

Simple sequin techniques

Sequins come in a variety of sizes and shapes and many different colours. They can be round, drop or oval and flat or saucer-shaped, and purchased singly or in ready-strung lengths.

Make sure that the hole in the sequin is large enough to take the eye of the needle and use spun nylon or ordinary sewing thread to stitch the sequins in place.

To apply sequins singly, tie a knot in the thread and push the needle through the fabric from the wrong side. Pull the thread through. Slip the sequin on to the needle and down the thread, level with the

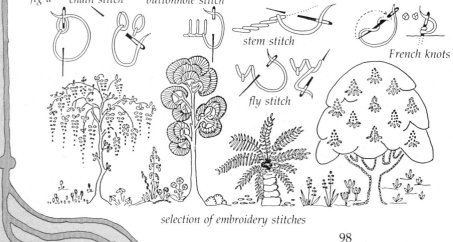

fig a　chain stitch　buttonhole stitch

stem stitch

French knots

fly stitch

selection of embroidery stitches

surface of the fabric. Push the needle through the fabric to the wrong side and secure the sequin. Either fasten off securely or continue placing the sequins in position as required, (see Fig d), overlapping each sequin to cover the centre hole as shown.

fig d

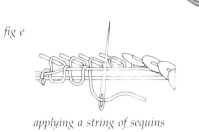

applying a single sequin

To apply sequins in a length, they have already been strung so that the holes overlap, so it is not necessary to work into each individual sequin. Tie a knot in the thread and push the needle through the fabric from the wrong side. Place the string of sequins in position on the right side of the fabric and sew over the thread between each sequin, (see Fig e).

fig e

applying a string of sequins

Below: *This quilted jacket is the perfect choice for evening wear. See pages 100 and 101 for instructions.*

Black quilted jacket

This design is for an experienced dressmaker, although the instructions give an indication of the cutting out and assembling of the pieces. This model fits an 86-91cm/34-36in bust size.

Materials

Fabric: silk crepe for painting 140cm/55in by 220cm/86½in; red silk crepe for the lining 140cm/55in by 200cm/78¾in; pongé No 5 for backing material 180cm/70¾in by 91cm/36in; 4m/4yd of black piping; 300cm/118in by 100cm/39½in synthetic padding material; white sequins; small and large white pearls; green cylindrical beads.

Paints: black, carmine red, scarlet, olive green, leaf green, chrome yellow and combinations of these colours as well as diluted versions.

Gutta: black, colourless.

Method examples

Use black gutta for the outside edges of the motifs and colourless gutta for the inside. Prepare large quantities of all the colours so that you can paint the motifs on the left and right sides at the same time. Also prepare lots of black.

Shade the flowers well, darkening the base of the petals to give some depth. Use a range of greens and yellows for the leaves.

To make up

Cut the painted silk according to the pattern and cutting instructions. Also cut out the red lining, allowing 2cm/¾in extra for seams.

Assemble the 2 back panels, lining up the design in the centre. Line up the patterns on the back and fronts at the shoulders and join.

On the reverse side of the assembled painted silk, place a layer of unseamed padding material cut to the same shape and size as the assembled painted silk, and then the pieces of pongé No 5, indicated by the shaded sections on the cutting instructions. If you have to add some extra padding material, match up the two pieces, butting the edges together so that the depth of fabric is the same over the entire surface. The padding material should be spread evenly over the whole jacket, without any seams. Tack the three layers to keep them together. To pad, stitch round the gutta contours, padding the motifs lightly with cotton wool. Sew on the sequins, pearls and beads and embroider the centre of the red flowers, and the white flowers as shown.

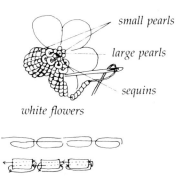

small pearls

large pearls

sequins

white flowers

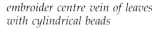

embroider centre vein of leaves with cylindrical beads

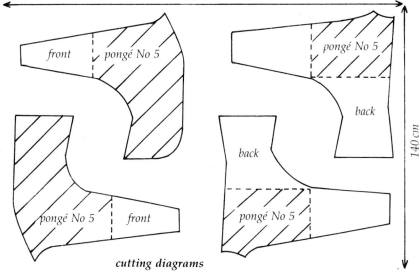

220 cm

front ⋎ *pongé No 5*

pongé No 5

back

pongé No 5 *front*

back

pongé No 5

140 cm

cutting diagrams

Fix the padding and pongé No 5 to the surface with large stitches vertically and horizontally in lines, about 5cm/2in apart, so that the padding doesn't tear.

Assemble and seam the side edges. Assemble red lining. Insert the piping between the lining and the padded silk on cuffs and outside edges of the jacket. Stitch round the outer edges of the lining, jacket and lower sleeve edges, leaving an opening of about 20cm/8in at the bottom of the back so that you can turn the jacket right side out. Finish the back opening.

On the red lining, embroider little flowers in knot stitch to fix the lining and the padding. Be careful not to catch in the outside layer of silk as you sew.

flowers for lining

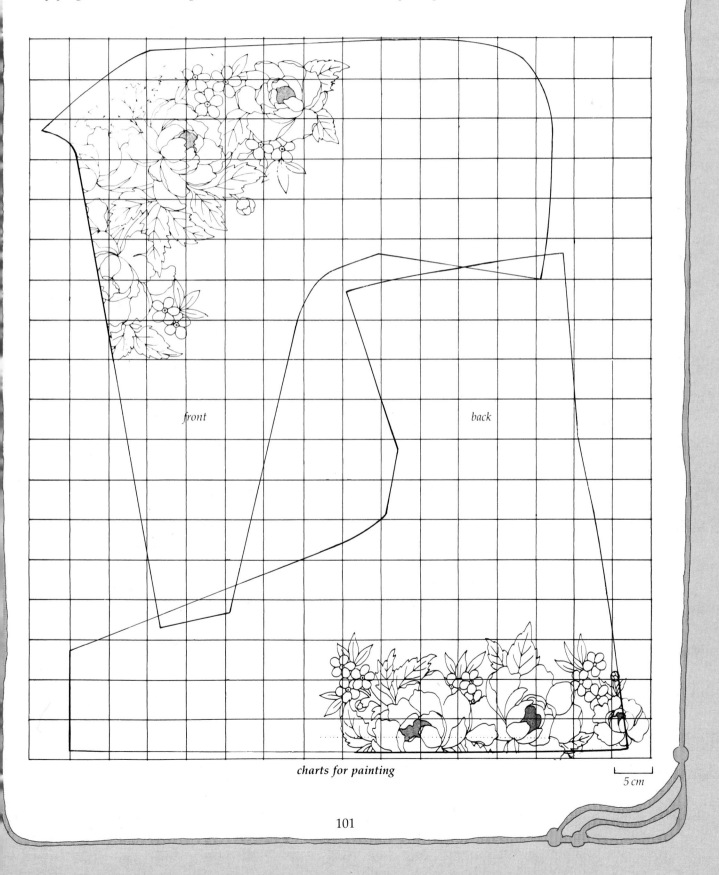

front

back

charts for painting

5 cm

101

Buttoned quilted jacket

You will need a suitable pattern to make this jacket as the instructions do not include any details of cutting out or assembling the pieces.

Materials

Fabric: silk satin sufficient to suit your own dressmaking pattern; lining and padding; buttons as required.

Paints: wine red, dark brown, rosewood, tangerine, Prussian blue, duck egg blue and combinations of these colours as well as diluted versions.

Gutta: beige; mix some scarlet and a little black with the gutta.

Method examples

Reproduce the flower drawing only on the sleeves. Use half the drawing on each side of the front, making sure the bird motifs are centred on either side. Use the whole design for the back.

The background is painted in bands; dark brown for the lower edge, then dark brown and a little lightly diluted tangerine for the next band up, then tangerine and

a little dark brown diluted for the next band, then diluted dark brown and, finally, tangerine with a touch of dark brown, both very diluted.

Paint the flowers in wine red, tinted with a little dark brown at the base and shaded lighter at the top. Paint the veins in pure wine red while the surface is still wet. The stalks are wine red.

Use varying shades of blue for the birds, tinted with a little wine red very diluted.

4 cm

Flowered quilted jacket

This design is for an experienced dressmaker and the instructions do not include precise details of the cutting out and assembling of the pieces. This model fits an 86-91cm/34-36in bust size.

Materials

Fabric: brocade silk, 2 lengths about 70cm/27½in wide by required length for body; 2 lengths about 46cm/18in wide by required length for sleeves; lining and padding to fit same measurements; about 4m/4yd of piping.

Paints: tangerine, wine red, ruby red, black, rosewood, dark brown, old gold and combinations of these colours as well as diluted versions.

Gutta: blue, red, yellow.

Method examples

Trace the design on to the silk. Vary the colour of the gutta to suit the flowers. Shade the flowers well and paint the tips of the petals tangerine.

Shade the lily in orange tones, more or less diluted and mixed with old gold or rosewood. The buds are half grey, half beige.

Use black diluted with water and alcohol for the background.

To make up

Assemble and pad the jacket, then line and pipe with grey satin.

Opposite: Vertical lines of quilting have been added to this striking jacket.

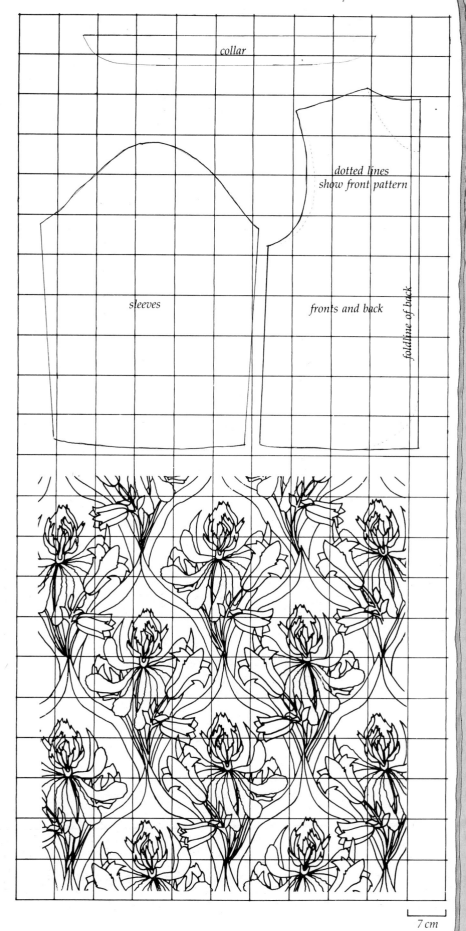

collar

dotted lines show front pattern

sleeves

fronts and back

foldline of back

7 cm

Quilted jacket

The instructions do not include details for cutting out or assembling the pieces of this jacket. It is worth finding a pattern perfectly suited to your own measurements to show off this bold and beautiful design.

Materials

Fabric: damask silk sufficient to suit your own dressmaking pattern; lining and padding.

Paints: rose pink, fuchsia, jade, duck egg blue, black, yellow-gold and combinations of these colours as well as diluted versions.

Gutta: colourless, black.

Method examples

Use the black gutta for the flowers and the colourless gutta for the leaves.

Shade the flowers well; they should be darker at the centre, (fuchsia and a little black), and then range from fuchsia to bright pink to almost white. Shade the leaves in diluted jade and diluted duck egg blue and jade, tinted with diluted yellow. Mix small amounts of these colours with grey and apply. Vary the colour of the veins. Use pure black for the background.

4 cm

Pullover and matching scarf

This exciting design features an elegant 'lady' motif appliqued on the pullover, with the same motif painted on the scarf.

The pullover can be adapted to fit any size and the model shown fits an 86-91cm/34-36in bust size.

Materials

Fabric: for the pullover, pongé No 9, allowing total width of 150cm/59in and 2 lengths of 73cm/28¾in, (or as required), and the same amount of fine jersey for lining; length of machine-ribbed jersey edging; oddments of fake fur, feathers, sequins, pearls.

For the scarf, pongé No 9, 91cm/36in square.

Paints: black, ruby red, Parma violet, rust and combinations of these colours as well as diluted versions.

Gutta: colourless, black, gold.

Method examples for pullover and scarf

Outline the hair, eyebrows and lashes in black gutta.

To paint the face, wet the areas that are to remain pale with water so that the colours spread slowly, then paint in very diluted rust.

Paint the eyelids and the hat in Parma violet and ruby red. When the surface of the silk is almost dry, paint in the base of the nose and the edge of the nostril with the same mix.

When the paint is completely dry, draw the veil carefully with black gutta and the sequins with gold gutta.

To make up pullover

Cut out the silk to the size required. Embroider the ring on the glove and the design along the arm with sequins and pearls. The earrings and necklace are also made from sewn-on pearls. Attach some feathers over the painted area, a piece of fur to the lady's collar, and small gold sequins to the bottom of the veil.

Assemble the front, back and sleeves. Sew the underarm and shoulder seams, adding the ribbed border inset at the shoulders.

Cut out the lining to match and assemble, then sew in place.

Lightly pad the contours of the face, hair and hat, using small running stitches.

Cut a 3cm/1¼in bias band and sew on to the neckline from one edge of ribbing to the other folding and sewing the bottom edge by hand. Sew a ribbed border 5cm/2in wide to the wrists and along the lower edge of the pullover, stretching as much as possible.

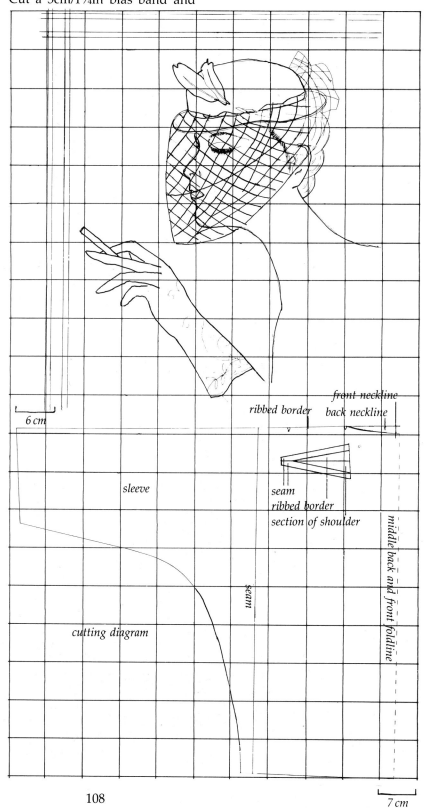

6 cm

front neckline

back neckline

ribbed border

sleeve

seam

ribbed border

section of shoulder

middle back and front foldline

seam

cutting diagram

7 cm

Eagle pullover

The body of the eagle is painted and the feathers are appliqued on this very striking pullover.

This design is for an experienced needlewoman and fits an 86-91cm/34-36in bust size.

Materials

Fabric: pongé No 9 a total of 235cm/92in by 76cm/30in wide, and the same amount of fine jersey for lining; 150cm/59in pongé No 9 for the feathers; gold embroidery thread; elastic; 2 buttons for cuffs.

Paints: Indian brown, Venetian red, chrome yellow, black, ruby red, tangerine and combinations of these colours as well as diluted versions.

Gutta: colourless.

Method examples

Paint the head, body and tail of the eagle in Venetian red, darkened here and there with Indian brown. For the tail, apply water to the area that is to remain white, so that the Indian brown spreads slowly.

The background is painted in slightly diluted tangerine, mixed with Venetian red.

Use gutta to mark out the pattern shape of the wings, shown by the thick line on the diagram. To paint the silk feathers, see chart Fig 1.

To make up

Cut out the silk according to the pattern. The feathers are 10cm/4in and 15cm/6in square, as shown on the chart. Using the illustrations as a guide, fold and sew the feathers by machine with a zig-zag stitch, then press. Stitch in place on the front of the pullover with gold embroidery thread along the centre folds, beginning with the innermost row of the wings. Complete the inner edge of each wing with gold chain stitches or narrow braid.

Join the shoulder seams. Assemble the front, back and sleeves. Join the side seams. Assemble the lining in the same way and attach this to the pullover. Cut a 3cm/1¼in bias band and stitch in place round the neckline.

Cut 2 cuffs 25cm/9¾in long by 10cm/4in wide, allowing an overlap. Cut out a slit for the wrists and neaten the edges with a 2cm/¾in bias edging. Stitch the cuffs in place making small, regular pleats along the edge of the sleeves.

Cut a band 5cm/2in wide and the required length to fit round the lower edge of the pullover. Stitch to the edge of the pullover and fold to the wrong side to form a casing for the elastic, leaving an opening. Insert the elastic and close the opening.

Opposite: Applique plummage is added to the painted eagle motif featured on this warm pullover. The feathers are outlined with gold embroidery. See overleaf for charts.

fig 1	10 cm×10 cm squares	number	15 cm × 15 cm squares	number
inside of wing	very pale Venetian red	16	mix Venetian red and pale Indian brown clear Indian brown slightly diluted Indian brown	6 8 4
outside of wing:	clear Indian brown	16	slightly diluted Indian brown clear Indian brown	8 1

assembling feathers

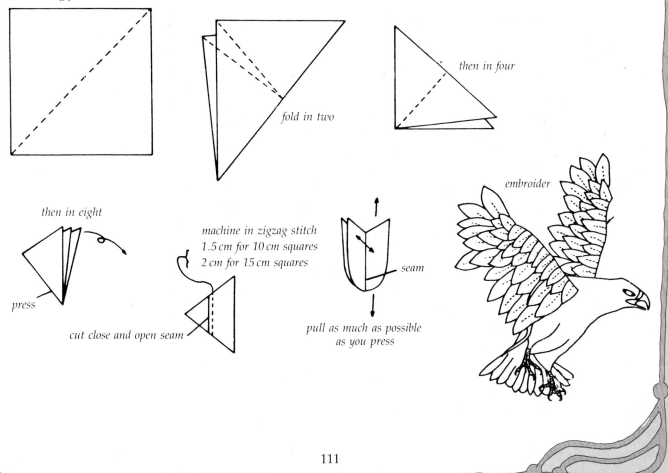

fold in two

then in four

then in eight

press

machine in zigzag stitch
1.5 cm for 10 cm squares
2 cm for 15 cm squares

cut close and open seam

seam

pull as much as possible
as you press

embroider

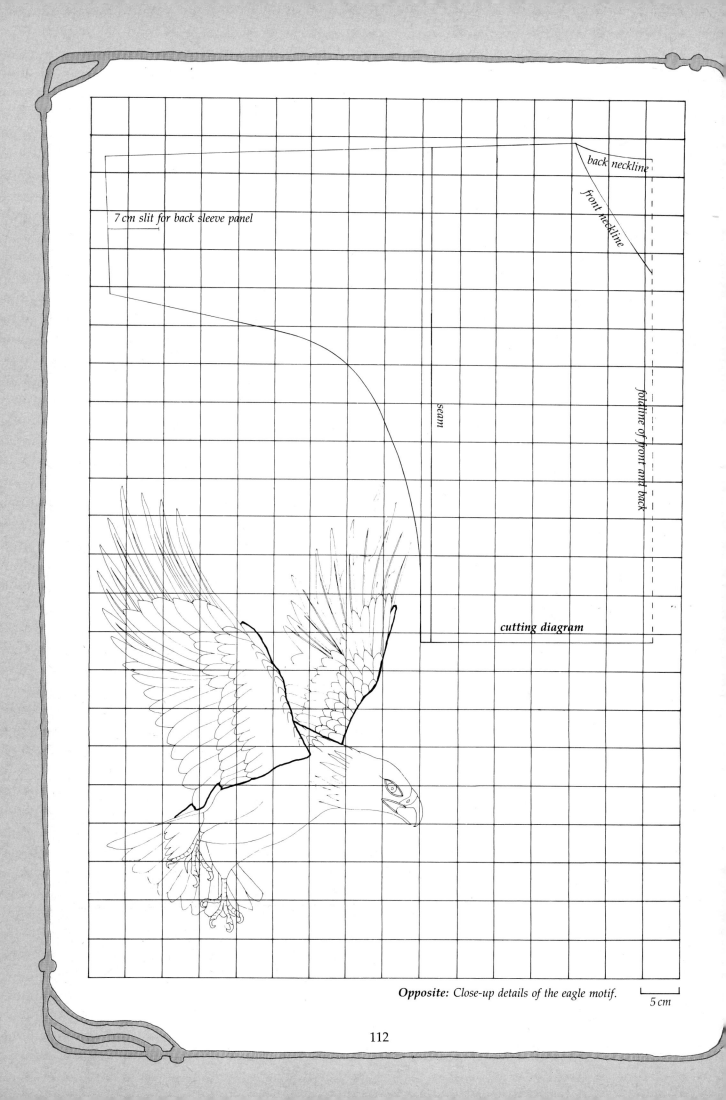

7 cm slit for back sleeve panel

back neckline

front neckline

seam

foldline of front and back

cutting diagram

Opposite: *Close-up details of the eagle motif.*

5 cm

How to begin

Once you have mastered the basic technique, this exciting craft can be used to produce luxurious and original fashion garments at relatively low costs.

There are three different methods used in painting on silk; gutta or resist, watercolour, and salt or alcohol techniques. The gutta or resist method can be used on its own to produce very simple, stylised motifs in a single colour. The watercolour method can also be used alone for very muted, abstract designs where one colour flows into another. Most designs, however, are based on a combination of these first two methods. Salt, or alcohol, is applied to a completed painting to give a stippled effect to certain areas, but these are not used as separate methods. Both agents affect the density of the paint colour; salt will darken it in mottled areas and alcohol lighten it.

Before attempting to paint on silk it is important to appreciate that you will never be able to reproduce an exact replica of any illustrated design. Silk is a natural fibre and, much like wool, varies in quality and texture. Paints may also vary in thickness and colour from one manufacturer to another. Another point to bear in mind is that a design may originally have been drawn free-hand, without any clear lines of reference, so it is a 'one-off', not to be repeated. These factors, however, greatly add to the fascination of this craft, as you will always produce your own unique design.

Make sure you have everything you will require to hand before beginning any project. You will need to work quickly to achieve satisfactory results and if you have to break off in the middle of an operation because you have forgotten to buy a brush fine enough to paint small areas, the whole process could be ruined. You will also need a steady hand and eye, so make sure you are not interrupted once you have commenced a painting!

You need not make any vast initial outlay on tools or materials. Scraps of silk can be found on most remnant counters at prices to suit all purses. Keep to a few basic paint colours for your first project. Don't go to the expense of purchasing a frame for a small item; you may already possess an embroidery frame which would make a suitable alternative. Or, if you can handle a screwdriver, it is a simple matter to make a fixed frame to any size.

Basic equipment

The tools required for painting on silk are easily obtainable from art and craft shops, or by mail order from specialist suppliers. The beginner's kit should contain the following:

A wooden frame, fixed or adjustable

Tracing paper

Silk fabric

Silk paints in two or three colours

Small white mixing cups and a container for water

Gutta, or resist agent, or water-solvent resist agent

Paper cones or resist applicators

Gutta or resist colourants, or coloured resist

Thinner and fixing agents, as recommended by the manufacturer of the range of paints being used

Special salt from silk paints suppliers, or fine or coarse cooking salt

Ethyl rubbing alcohol

Two or three soft watercolour-type brushes

Pencil and white eraser fluid

Push pins or three-point thumbtacks

Ruler

Adhesive tape

Cotton wool or cotton buds

Scissors

Opposite: Some of the basic equipment used in painting on silk.

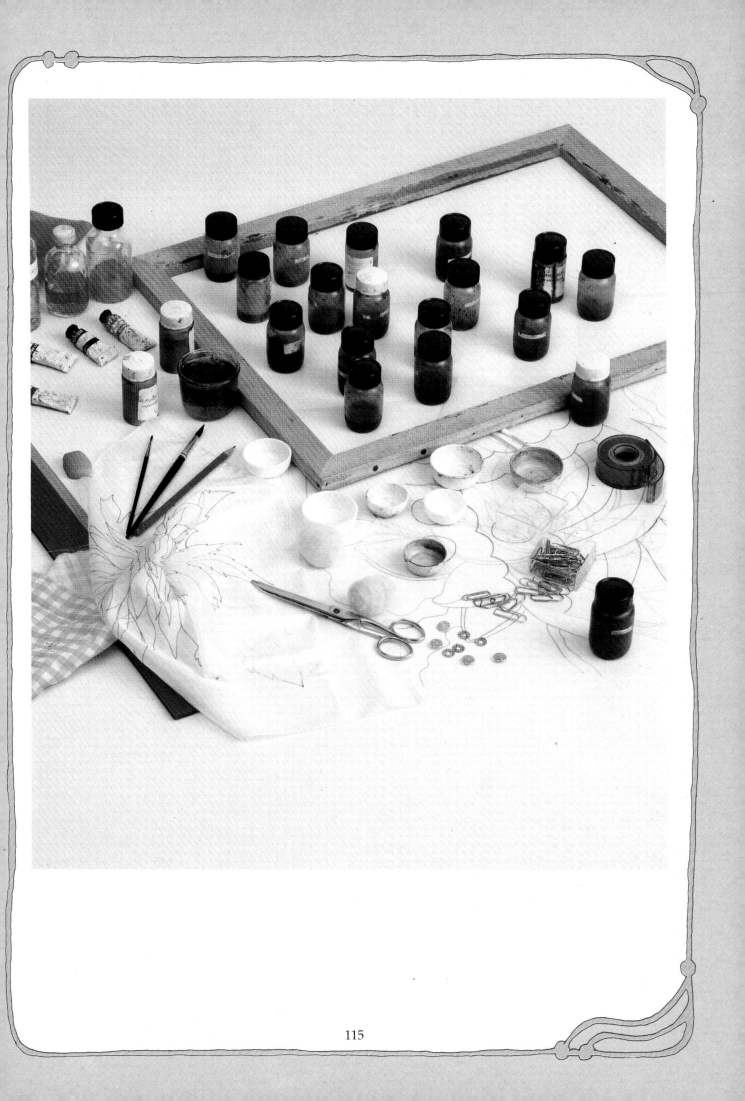

Tools, materials and basic techniques

This chapter gives details of the items and basic resist and watercolour techniques needed to begin your first venture into silk painting. Any additional material, or special methods needed to complete individual projects featured in this book, will be given in the instructions for the design.

Silk fabrics

Silk is obtained from the cocoon of the wild or cultivated silkworm and, when these are dried, 31g/1oz will provide sufficient thread for 7 metres/yards of a lightweight fabric 90cm/35½in wide.

The Chinese have a system of weight gauge for silk, referred to as a 'mommie', and this term is used universally in the wholesale silk trade to indicate the weight of a fabric. One mommie equals 4.3056gm/⁵⁄₃₂oz in weight to one square metre/yard of fabric; 6 mommie is considered a lightweight quality, suitable for scarves, but a heavier weight of 8 mommie is more appropriate for clothing. As a very general guide, anything under 10 mommie is considered to be a lightweight fabric; anything over is classed as a medium to heavyweight quality.

There are many different types of silk available but a lightweight silk lining material, called Habotai, is probably most widely used for silk painting. Tussah, a type of fabric produced by uncultivated silkworms, is more commonly known as 'wild silk'. Shantung is a mixture of wild and cultivated silk.

You can also obtain silk noil, twill, pongé, crepe de chine, crepe satin, taffeta, organza and crepe georgette but not all of these qualities are ideal for silk painting and many of them will impose their own very different characteristics on to a design. Heavily-textured silks, for instance, will not take the paints evenly and they also tend to encourage a 'bridge' when the gutta is applied. This will later allow the watercolours to break through the resist line and run into each other.

For the inexperienced painter lightweight silk is easier to work with because resists penetrate it more readily and paints flow better. For your first projects keep to white silk, as this background produces clear, brilliant colours when the paints are applied. An important point to remember is that white is not represented in any range of silk paint, so the white background of the fabric is used in many designs to highlight an area, or to define outlines between blocks of colours.

You may eventually wish to experiment with cream or pastel backgrounds. In this event, the chosen background colour will be the palest shade in a design and you will not be able to introduce any white. The background colour will also have an effect on the paints you use and it may be difficult to visualize the finished colouring of a design.

It is best to hand-wash silk before beginning to paint, to remove any traces of dressing or grease. Wash in hand-warm water, rinse well then roll the fabric into a towel smoothing out any creases. When it is still damp, iron with a warm iron. This procedure should also be adopted when laundering a completed article.

Frames

Silk can only be painted sucessfully if the fabric is evenly stretched and freely suspended. If you intend to work on items of a specific size, such as scarves it is best to use a fixed frame. If you plan to tackle projects of different sizes, such as blouses or lingerie, then it will be more practical to use a frame with adjustable tension.

Before any silk is stretched on to the frame, cover the frame with adhesive tape. It can then be easily wiped clean with a damp cloth and remains of paint from previous work will not spoil a new piece of silk.

To stretch the silk over the frame, use three-point architects' thumbtacks or push pins to secure it. The three-point tacks are particularly easy to remove and will not tear the silk.

On a fixed frame, begin by pinning the four corners in place, stretching the silk and keeping it parallel to the edges of the frame. Next, secure the middle of each side, then at intervals of no more than 5cm/2in round all the edges. The silk needs to be stretched evenly over the frame and as tightly as a drum.

To fix the silk to an adjustable frame, set the frame to the approximate dimensions of the silk you are using. Pin the fabric to the movable bar and then on to the parallel fixed bar. Continue as given for a fixed frame, placing the pins approximately 5cm/2in apart while you stretch the silk. To do this, release the two screws on the movable bar and gently pull to stretch. Do not pull too hard or you may rip the fabric. When you have obtained a taut stretch, tighten the screws.

Gutta or resist

The flow of paints is controlled by a product called 'resist' - a thick, colourless liquid sold in bottles or cans. When a thin line of resist is drawn on silk, it penetrates the fibres and stops the flow of the paints. There are two types of resist readily available; gutta, which is rubber-based, and a water-soluble resist. Both types should be shaken well before use.

The most popular way to apply gutta or resist for outlining a design is with a metal-tipped applicator bottle; water-soluble resist should only be applied by this means. A cone made of tracing paper is a suitable alternative for rubber-based gutta, but the success of this method will depend on the size of hole from which the gutta will be squeezed. When using an applicator, or a cone, it should be held like a pencil but do not slant it too much.

Making a cone: cut a rectangle 14 by 18cm/5½ by 7in from a piece of tracing paper. Begin by folding the paper at a 30 degree angle towards the top, then roll the paper round the triangle. Make sure that the hole at the tip is no larger than a fine needle or pin.

To close the cone, first roll a small piece of adhesive tape around the tip, making sure it does not go over the edge and block the hole. Close the remaining openings with tape, except for the top into which the gutta will be poured.

Consistency of resists: gutta is usually ready to use. It should not be too thick, which can happen when the solvent evaporates. To dilute, add a few drops of gutta solvent. Test gutta by dipping a toothpick into the liquid and holding it over a mixing cup; if the gutta forms a thin trickle, the consistency is right. Try it out on silk. Overly thick or thin gutta will not control the flow of paints. Moreover, overly thick gutta does not dry easily and will remain sticky. Water-soluble resist is ready to use and should not be diluted.

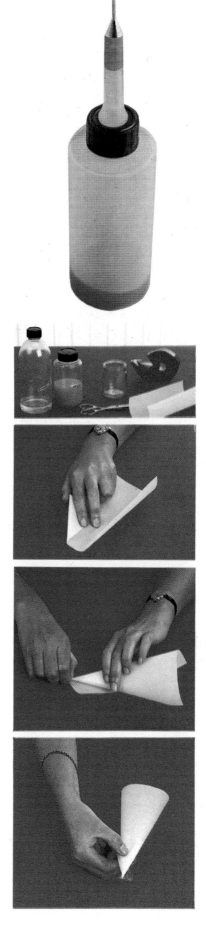

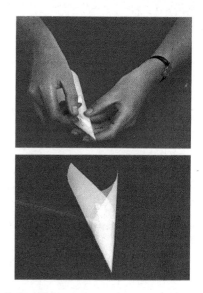

Colouring gutta: if you wish to obtain a bright colour, put a pea-sized drop of gutta colourant into a small bowl; use about quarter of that quantity for a pastel gutta. Dilute with a thimbleful of gutta solvent and add enough gutta to fill the applicator half full. Pour the mixture into the applicator if you are using a cone, seal it with tape.

Water-soluble resist can be discreetly coloured with only a few drops of silk paint.

Silk paints

For the projects in this book, we have used readily-available traditional silk paints. They may be diluted with a solution of 50% water and 50% ethyl rubbing alcohol, or use the special dilutant available for this purpose.

The colour chart shows pure colours which are labelled, and in the column on the right of each colour, diluted versions of the colours are shown. Colours of the same range can be mixed to create new colours or different tones and shades, for example, vermilion plus yellow equals orange. Colours from different ranges or from different manufacturers, however, should never be mixed. Also, it is not advisable to use gutta or fixatives of one make in combination with paints of another make.

Always test each colour on a sample strip of silk before using it directly on your project. Use white containers to mix your paints.

Quantities of paint needed: it is important to estimate ahead how much paint you will need, particularly for large even areas and when mixing colours. The heavier the silk, the more paint it will absorb. For example, to cover the background on one square metre/yard of 6 mommie silk you will need about 40gm/2oz of paint but for the same background on twill, you will need approximately double this quantity.

Blending paints: there are two ways of accomplishing this within an area which has been treated with resist.

1) Use paints straight out of the bottle. Place the different colours you have chosen side by side, by dipping your brush directly into one of the bottles, rinsing, then dipping it into the next, and so on. Work fast, so that the surface does not dry. If you want a lighter area, leave it white. While the surface is still wet, rinse the brush again, pick up a small amount of the water/alcohol solution and use that over the entire surface, rubbing it a little to allow the colours to blend.

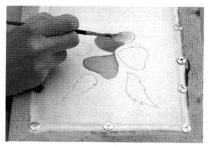

2) If you are working with a large area and you are concerned about being able to paint quickly with different colours, prepare the paints in small containers instead. In some cases only a few drops will be sufficient. Apply the paints side by side, allowing them to intermix, without rinsing the brush as you go along. Avoid using too many containers and colours, so as not to become confused or have a lot of waste.

Textile paints: these paints are creamy in consistency and are set with an iron. When used without water they do not bleed on the fabric. They can be used to high-

light certain details in a design.

Anti-fusant: traditional silk paints flow into each other on a fabric which has not been treated with resist outlines. An interesting new way to paint while having a certain level of control is with an anti-fusant. You can buy this produce ready for use, or prepare it yourself by mixing 20% gutta with 80% ethyl rubbing alcohol.

Shake the liquid well, spread over the entire area where you wish to avoid bleeding with a brush especially reserved for this purpose and rinsed in alcohol, then allow to dry. A thin layer is all that is needed. Pick up a small amount of paint with a separate brush and apply over the anti-fusant. The paints will not bleed. Use this method for fine detailed painting without resist. Use different shapes of brushes to obtain a great variety of effects.

Proceed as usual after painting with steam setting and washing.

The anti-fusant will come out and the fabric will retain its free-hand painted design.

Brushes

Use a brush to apply paints to silk. Your brushes should be of good quality but not necessarily sable brushes. One fine brush and a thicker one will be sufficient for your needs. To cover large surfaces with the same colour, rather than a brush use a piece of cotton wool soaked in the required colour. Special foam brushes and foam applicators can also be used.

Painting backgrounds: once paints are applied to silk, they dry very quickly. To obtain an even background *never* go back over a dry area with a wet brush, or place wet paint next to dry paint if there is no resist to separate them. You would then have a dark edge line which is usually difficult, if not impossible to correct.

You must therefore work quickly and to cover large surfaces use foam brushes. Remember to have a fine brush handy for filling in any nooks and crannies you may have missed. See to it that the surface remains wet. Where there is a central design, paint alternately on both sides of this, so as to keep both sides wet.

Fixing the paints

Once the painting is completed, the colours must be 'set' so that they will not run in laundering, or fade with exposure to light – this process is referred to as 'fixing'.

Prior to fixing, the painted silk is extremely fragile and must be handled carefully. It is sensitive to water, alcohol and light. Three methods of fixing can be used but follow the paint manufacturer's instructions and remember that you must never mix different types of paint and fixatives.

1) Brush-on fixative: for some ranges of paint the manufacturers recommend a fixative in liquid form. This is brushed on after the paints are dry with a broad, stiff brush – make sure all the fabric is well covered. Leave to dry for one hour or the period of time recommended by the manufacturer.

Remove the fabric from the frame and handwash in *cold water*. During this process some surplus dye may be removed, as well as any gutta used. Hang up to dry and, finally, iron. The colours should now be permanent and set for handwashing (30°C or 86°F) and some methods of dry-cleaning.

2) Iron-setting paints: some water-based paints can be fixed by using an iron set to the temperature recommended by the manufacturer.

After the paints are dry, remove the silk from the frame, taking care that it does not touch any damp surface. Iron the silk all over the 'wrong' side. If the recommended iron temperature is too high for the fabric, protect it with a piece of plain white paper between the iron and the fabric. This method will set the colours permanently for handwashing.

3) Steam-setting paints: alcohol-based paints are best fixed by steaming in accordance with the manufacturers' instructions The combination of heat and steam locks the colours into the fabric. Purpose-built steam ovens are available but are rather expensive. As an alternative, it is possible to use a pressure-cooker.

After the paints have dried for some hours, remove the fabric from the frame and roll it very carefully into a larger piece of absorbent paper; white blotting paper or wall-paper liner are ideal. Paper with a shiny surface will not allow the steam to penetrate. The silk must be absolutely flat, with no wrinkles or creases and must not overlap or touch itself. Roll the paper and silk into a sausage-shape of about 4cm/1½in diameter. Close the roll with masking tape, or adhesive tape, then curve it into a wreath shape and also seal the ends.

Wrap the roll loosely in aluminium foil. The fabric must be protected in such a way that steam can reach it, but no water can come into contact with it. Partly fold the ends of the parcel to allow steam to enter but prevent condensation running into the centre of the parcel, so damaging the painted silk. Fill the pressure cooker with 2cm/¾in of water, or not quite to the base of the perforated basket, (see Figs a and b). Fit the foil-wrapped parcel, folded ends facing downwards, into the basket without touching the sides; place the basket on the trivet inside the pressure-cooker. Moisture will condense on the lid and if drops of water fall on to the packet they may penetrate and form water spots on the fabric. To avoid this, before closing the pressure-cooker, take a piece of aluminium foil, shape it into a dome and place it over the packet. Close the lid. Raise the pressure to 2.3kg/5lb per square 2.5cm/1in and steam for about 45–60 minutes. Remove the packet and allow to cool.

If a pressure-cooker is not available, use a large pot with a well-fitting lid but treble the fixing time. Do not allow the pot to boil dry!

fig a shows the inside of a pressure cooker

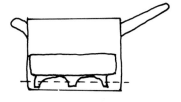

fig b shows the level of water in the bottom of the cooker

Salt and alcohol techniques

Once the painting has been completed and prior to fixing the paints, marvellous mottled and spotted effects can be achieved by either applying salt to certain areas while the silk is still wet, or alcohol when the silk is dry. These techniques can also be combined in one design.

With both techniques, discretion is best. Be careful not to use too much salt and scatter it well, otherwise you may get a muddled effect. Use a small brush to apply the alcohol, pick up a small amount and then blot your brush before beginning. The alcohol spreads quickly – you can always add more but you cannot take away!

Humidity plays a role in these techniques. With the salt, be sure it is completely dry for maximum effect and that the fabric is wet. With the alcohol, the fabric must be completely dry to produce a mottled effect.

Salt technique: this consists of scattering various kinds of salt over a wet surface. You can use coarse salt, table salt or salt crystals. Each grain of salt will attract the paint towards it by absorbing the water. The result is a lovely spotted effect which is completely unpredictable.

Alcohol technique: this is obtained by placing a brush dipped in alcohol on to a dry painted surface. The alcohol repulses the colour and thereby produces light coloured spots, surrounded by an outline of concentrated colour.

Above: *Applying salt to a wet fabric.*
Below: *Applying alcohol to a dry fabric.*

Opposite: *The effects achieved with salt technique.*

How to enlarge or reduce a design

The previous pages in this book give diagrams of designs and motifs which you can copy. To enable them to fit into the page size they have been considerably reduced and to produce the size indicated in the instructions, the design must be traced out to the measurements given on the squared grid. As an example, if the measurement for one square of a grid is given as 3cm/1¼in and the design covers ten squares, the finished size of the painting will be 30cm/11¾in, (see Figs a and b). For conversions from centimetres to inches, see page 4.

You may, of course, wish to enlarge the actual drawing still further, or even reduce it, and there are several ways which will enable you to obtain an exact copy. Various forms of photocopiers will enlarge or reduce a diagram on paper and more sophisticated machines will copy a design to any size, on any material, but these are rather costly.

The simplest way to enlarge or reduce a drawing, however, is to use a pantograph, which you can either make yourself, or obtain from most art or craft shops, (see Fig c). A pantograph consists of four flattened rods, or pieces of wood. At the appropriate points, a tracing point is fixed to these rods for tracing over the lines of the original, and a drawing point for making the copy. The pantograph is hinged at the crossing points and can be adjusted to enlarge or reduce the copy.

fig a

design for enlarging

fig b

3 cm

enlarged design to correct measurements

fig c

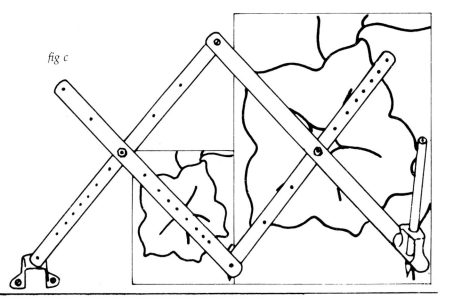

drawing of a pantograph

How to transfer designs on to silk

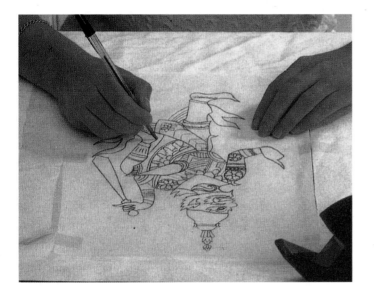

Once you have produced a drawing to the correct size needed for the design you have in mind, there are two ways of transferring it on to the silk.

1) Place tracing paper over the drawing and trace over the outlines with a heavy, waterproof marker. With the silk stretched tightly over the frame, place the traced design under the silk and hold it lightly in position with adhesive tape at the corners. Outline the design directly with resist, then remove the taped tracing and proceed to paint.

2) For greater precision, trace the design with a pencil on the wrong side of the tracing paper. Place the tracing paper wrong side down over the silk, which is placed flat on a table, and go over all the outlines again. The pencil lines will show lightly on the silk and when the silk is stretched over the frame, you will be able to outline the design with resist.

Problems with gutta and corrections

TYPE OF PROBLEM	REASONS	CORRECTIONS
The lines of gutta are too wide and uneven, with a 'blob' at the beginning and the end. Poor control.	The gutta is flowing too fast because the opening is too wide.	– Make a new paper cone with a smaller hole. – Place a small piece of paper at the start and the end of a line to catch the 'blob' or starting drop. This is especially useful when using an applicator.
Spots of gutta.	– The silk is not tautly stretched and touches the work surface; the lines spread and smear. – The cone is not tightly closed or you are squeezing too hard which allows the gutta to escape. – The applicator is not tightly closed.	– Stretch the silk again. – Make a new cone or seal the cracks with tape. – The gutta does not come out of the cone or applicator because it is too thick. Add some gutta solvent and place into a fresh cone. If the hole is too small; enlarge it with a needle. – You have placed too much gutta in the cone. Empty it and fill again.
The gutta does not work effectively, paints breach the dam and jump the line of resist.	– The gutta is too thick. – The gutta did not completely penetrate the fabric. – The gutta is too liquid. – The gutta is of poor quality.	– Prepare another cone and add more solvent to the gutta. – Add more solvent to the gutta and use a new cone. On heavier fabrics it might be necessary to apply the gutta on the reverse side. – Open the cone, allow the solvent to evaporate from the gutta and use a new cone.
The gutta has breaks in the line and paints run through the openings.	– You have left openings, however tiny, in the lines. – The applicator skipped on the silk while you were applying the gutta and has created an uneven line.	– Be sure you have good lighting where you work and go over the openings again before you proceed to paint. – The tape may have gone beyond the tip of the cone, make another cone. – You have been pushing too hard on the silk, use a lighter touch. – You are working against the grain of the silk. Try to move with the fibres.

Problems with paints and corrections

TYPE OF PROBLEM	REASONS	CORRECTIONS
Background colours are uneven and they streak or have dark edge areas.	– You have diluted your paints too much and they are unstable. – Your brush was not clean. – There is too much water and not enough alcohol in your mixed paint.	– Try a special product for diluting paints, it helps to avoid streaking. – Clean all your tools very well. – Modify your mixed paint by using different proportions of water + alcohol.
Backgrounds are uneven, the colours show dark edge lines and light spots.	– You went back over a dry area. – You applied fresh paint next to dry paint.	The fabric should always remain wet while you are working.
Spot of colour on a white surface.	– Clumsiness – Gap in the gutta line.	– Check the gutta and close the opening in the line if necessary. – Clean the spot with a cotton swab dipped in alcohol while you place a cotton ball underneath.
Spot on an area which has already been painted.	– Clumsiness – Gap in the gutta line	– If the spot is located within a small area, moisten the entire area again with a brush dipped in alcohol and rub where the spot is. Remove as much paint as possible from the edges with a drier brush. Repeat this operation several times then apply paint again. – If the spot is on a large surface, there is not much you can do about it. In general you can save a background with a problem by: 1. Moistening the entire area and scattering coarse salt. 2. Using alcohol to add spots thus masking the problem.

Index

If readers have difficulty obtaining any of the materials or equipment mentioned in this book, please write for further information to the publishers,
Search Press Ltd., Wellwood, North Farm Road, Tunbridge Wells, Kent TN2 3DR, England

If you are interested in any other of the art and craft titles published by Search Press please send for free colour catalogue to:
Search Press Ltd, Dept B, Wellwood, North Farm Road, Tunbridge Wells, Kent TN2 3DR.